ALL ABOUT ALCL3 FOR N-HETEROARENES

DR. RAJNIKANTH SUNKE
DR. S. K. MOODAPELLY

To the Beloved Parents

Contents

Foreword

This book is to give a knowledge about the recent review on N-Heteroarenes synthesis using AlCl3 reagent.

Preface

N-heteroarenes are considered as a privileged class of heterocyclic compounds that has not only found enormous applications in Medicinal Chemistry / Pharmaceutical Chemistry and drug discovery but also in other areas of Chemistry.[1] This class of compounds has ability to attain the required pharmacological, pharmacokinetic, toxicological, and physicochemical properties necessary for the drug candidates to become the ultimate drugs. It is therefore not surprising that a large number of drugs currently available for patient's use belong to this class.

Acknowledgements

For the Guidance of **Manojit Pal**, *Department of Medicinal Chemistry, Dr. Reddy's Institute of Life Sciences, University of Hyderabad Campus, Gachibowli, Hyderabad 500 046, India.*

Prologue

Use of AlCl$_3$ beyond Friedel Crafts alkylation / acylation reaction: An overview on the development of unique methodologies leading to *N*-heteroarenes

CHAPTER I

Abstract

As a privileged class of heterocyclic compounds N-heteroarenes has found enormous applications in many areas including medicinal / pharmaceutical chemistry and drug discovery. Consequently, a wide variety of methods have been reported for their synthesis. While not free from their own limitations the $AlCl_3$ mediated methods appeared to have some particular advantages in preparing a number of useful N-heteroarenes. Besides the famous Friedel–Crafts (FC) alkylation / acylation reactions one such example is $AlCl_3$-induced heteroarylation of arenes and heteroarenes that can be used to prepare certain class of N-heteroarenes in an operationally simple, efficient and cost effective manner. However, no systematic and detailed study regarding application potential on this method was performed till 2002. Some other examples that emerged in the recent past include $AlCl_3$ induced heteroarylation-cyclization, hydroarylation-heteroarylation, sulfonyl group migration etc. All these innovative methodologies allowed the direct access to several unique and novel N-heteroarenes some of which showed interesting pharmacological properties including anti-inflammatory, anti-cancer and antibacterial activities when tested in vitro. While unlike FC reactions many of these $AlCl_3$ mediated methodologies are still in their initial stage of developments, a continuing effort to uncover their further potential in organic synthesis / medicinal chemistry is necessary. The current article provides an overview of these unique methodologies that highlights the use of $AlCl_3$ beyond FC reactions leading to new N-heteroarenes of biological significance.

CHAPTER II

Introduction: N–heteroarenes

N-heteroarenes are considered as a privileged class of heterocyclic compounds that has not only found enormous applications in Medicinal Chemistry / Pharmaceutical Chemistry and drug discovery but also in other areas of Chemistry.[1] This class of compounds has ability to attain the required pharmacological, pharmacokinetic, toxicological, and physicochemical properties necessary for the drug candidates to become the ultimate drugs. It is therefore not surprising that a large number of drugs currently available for patient's use belong to this class. Representative examples of some *N*-heteroarene based drugs are shown in Fig. 1. This class of compounds are continued to be attractive templates for the design and identification of novel new chemical entities (NCEs) and eventually discovery of new drugs.[2] Consequently, a wide variety of methods have been reported for their synthesis. The transition metal-mediated coupling reactions particularly based on C–C bond forming reactions have occupied the center stage in organic synthesis[3] due to their versatile nature, increased functional group toleration, and improved yields. This strategy has also been applied successfully to the synthesis of *N*-heteroarenes. One such strategy popularly known as Suzuki coupling[4] involving the use of a Pd-catalyst and arylboronic acids is being utilized extensively for this purpose. Similarly, the use of other organometallic reagents such as ArZnX (X = halide) in the presence of a Pd-catalyst has also been used.[5a,b] All these strategies have been found to be highly efficient and effective in synthesizing several *N*-heteroarene based bioactive compounds and marketed drugs.[5c] While undoubtedly being versatile especially for linking one heteroarene with another *via* a C-C bond forming reaction these methods often require the use of expensive catalysts / reagents or cumbersome preparation of boronic acids or organo-zinc reagents if not available commercially. Among the several other strategies explored for this purpose in the recent past, the uses of $AlCl_3$ have been found to be effective in certain cases particularly in the preparation of a particular class of heteroarenes. While not free from their own limitations the $AlCl_3$ mediated methods appeared to have some other advantages that can be handy in preparing a number of useful heteroarenes. The current review article will mainly cover the development of $AlCl_3$ mediated methodologies other than Friedel–Crafts reactions and their applications in synthesizing appropriate class of heteroarenes of pharmacological interest. Additionally, limitations and advantages of these emerging methodologies are discussed.

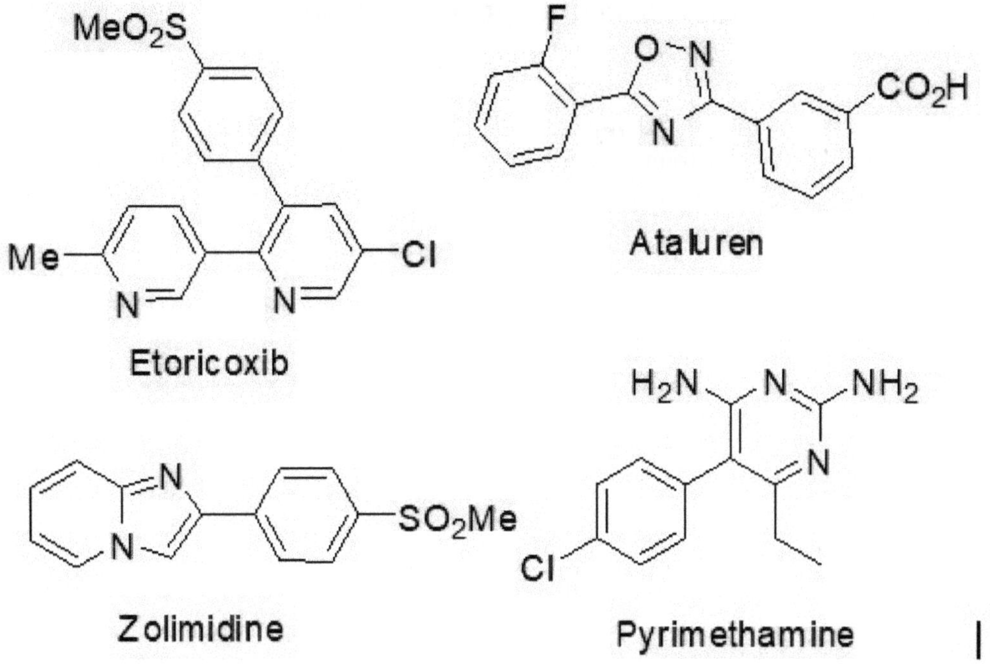

MeO$_2$S

Me

Cl

Etoricoxib

F

CO$_2$H

Ataluren

SO$_2$Me

Zolimidine

H$_2$N

NH$_2$

Cl

Pyrimethamine

Fig. 1. Representative examples of some *N*-heteroarene based drugs.

CHAPTER III

AlCl₃ in C-C bond forming reactions: Earlier developments

Aluminum, a group 13 element, is one of the most abundant metals in the earth's crust. As an inexpensive, less toxic and strong Lewis acid, AlCl$_3$ has found extensive applications in many organic transformations[6] One of the important applications of AlCl$_3$ in organic synthesis was observed way back in 1877 when Charles Friedel and James Crafts discovered a set of ground-breaking new reactions[7a] that were subsequently named as currently well-known Friedel–Crafts (FC) reactions.[7b] Among the two types of these reactions *i.e.* alkylation and acylation the latter category became a powerful tool for C-C bond forming reactions and found wide applications both in academic and industrial organizations. Even today Friedel–Crafts acylations appear to be the method of choice for the acylation of arenes and heteroarenes. While AlCl$_3$ has found several other applications in organic synthesis its use in the formation of a C-C bond between arenes and heteroarenes was reported in some isolated cases till 2002.For example, the AlCl$_3$ mediated reaction of 2-chloroquinoline or 4,7-dichloroquinoline or 2-chlorobenzothiazole with resorcinol or 4-chlororesorcinol was reported to give the dihydroxyphenyl- or chlorodihydroxyphenylquinoline and benzothiazole derivatives in 1952.[8a] Similarly, the reaction of 3,6-dichloropyridazine (**1**)with phenol derivatives in the presence of AlCl$_3$ was reported in 1966 that afforded 3-chloro-6-(2,4- and 2,5-dihydroxyphenyl)pyridazines (**2**, Scheme 1).[8b,c] Indeed, this strategy was used for the preparation of analogues of prizidilol with 4-alkoxy substituents in the phenyl ring.[8b] While, a 3-indolyl derivative (**3**, Scheme 1) was also prepared *via* the reaction of **1** with indole (as reported in 1990) the overall this strategy was found to be of very limited scope.[8c] In 1999, a facile synthesis of 4-acyl-6-aryl-2-oxo-2,3-dihydropyrimidines from 2,6-dichloropyrimidine-4-carbonyl chloride was described *via* a similar AlCl$_3$ mediated reaction.[9] All these reports prompted our group and others to explore the AlCl$_3$ mediated C-C bond forming reactions (other than FC alkylation / acylation reactions) as an unique strategy for accessing a variety of *N*-heteroarene based library of small molecules. It was beyond doubt that the success of FC reaction has been the real inspiration behind these efforts.

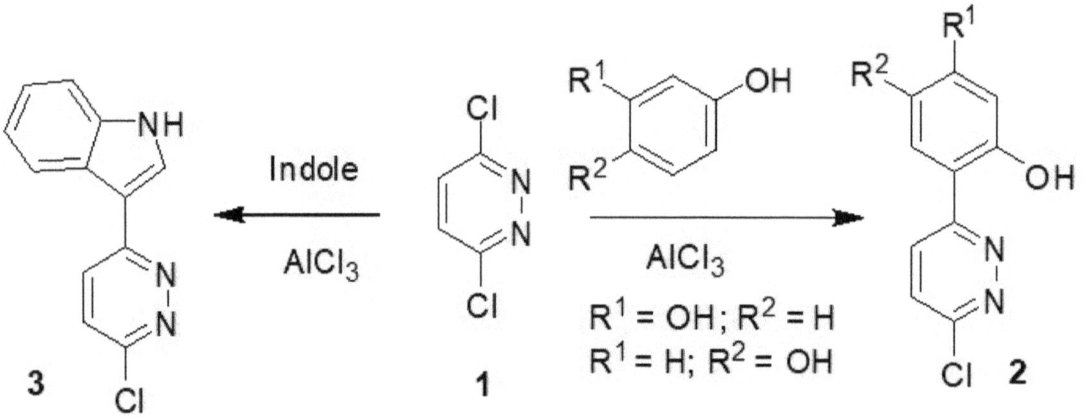

Scheme 1. AlCl$_3$ inducedreaction of **1** with phenols and indole

CHAPTER IV

Heteroarylation of arenes and heteroarenes

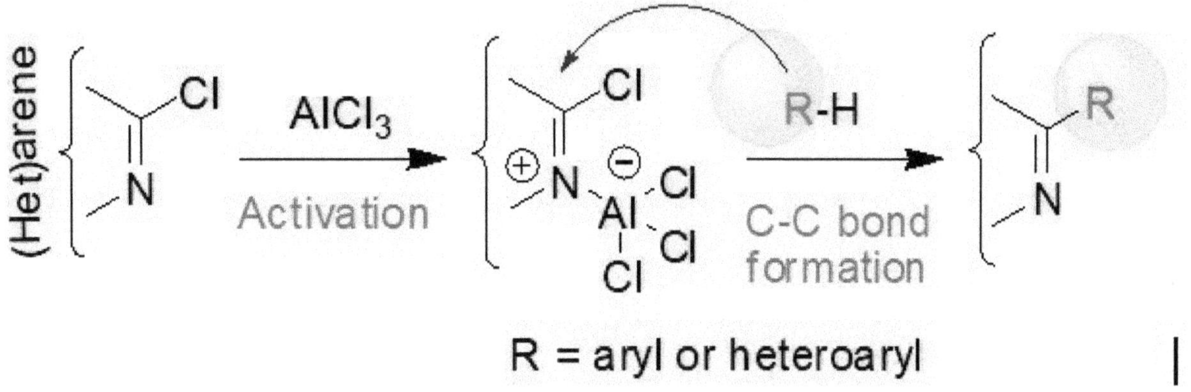

Scheme 2. A general representation on heteroarylation of arenes and heteroarenes

Introduction of a heteroaryl moiety on an arene or heteroarene ring is generally referred to as heteroarylation of arenes and heteroarenes (Scheme 2). Interestingly, a C-H bond of the arene or heteroarene ring is apparently cleaved and the "H" atom is replaced by the heteroaryl moiety during this process. Consequently, a C-C bond is formed to afford the heteroarylated product. While Scheme 1 could be an early example of this class of reactions mediated by $AlCl_3$ the potential of this strategy is being explored in recent time. An outline on the sequential development of this methodology is presented in the following sections.

CHAPTER V

Synthesis of pyrrolo[1,2-b]pyridazines

In 2002, as part of our ongoing in-house drug discovery program we became interested in constructing a small library of molecules based on 6,7-disubstituted pyrrolo[1,2-*b*]pyridazine framework. This work was motivated by the structural similarities of the target compounds with a non-xanthine adenosine A1 receptor antagonist[10] related to both diuretic and antihypertensive effects. Thus a systematic study was carried out on $AlCl_3$ induce heteroarylation of pyrrolo[1,2-*b*]pyridazines (**4**) to afford the desired products (**5**) one of which was further converted to a compound (**6**) of potential biological interest (Scheme 3).[11] While product yields were not particularly high in some cases the consistent ability of $AlCl_3$ to form C-C bond between two heteroarenes was noteworthy and remarkable. It was therefore necessary to understand the potential of this strategy and devote continuing effort for this purpose.

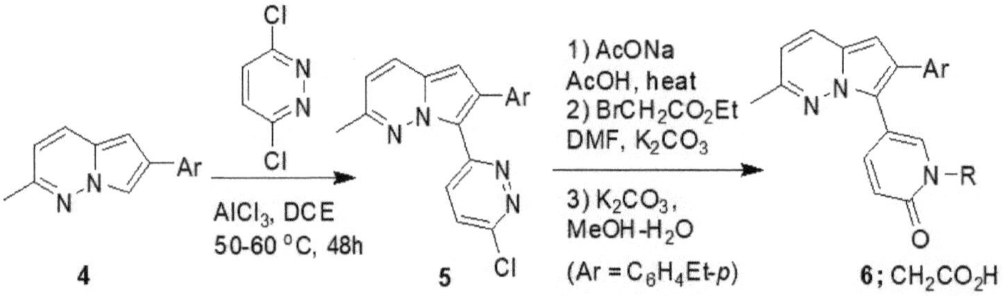

Ar = C_6H_4Me-*p* (**5a**, 65%); C_6H_4(i-Bu)-*p* (**5b**, 42%); C_6H_4Cl-*p* (**5c**, 50%), C_6H_3(di-OMe)-*o,p* (**5d**, 60%), C_6H_4F-*p* (**5e**, 71%), C_6H_3(F-*m*)(Me-*p*) (**5f**, 89%), C_6H_4Et-*p* (**5g**, 76%), C_6H_4OMe-*p* (**5h**, 93%), $C_6H_4NO_2$-*p* (**5i**, 72%), C_6H_4Me-*p* (**5j**, 20%)

Scheme 3. Synthesis of 6,7-disubstituted pyrrolo[1,2-*b*]pyridazines

CHAPTER VI

Synthesis of 4-substituted 2H-phthalazin-1-ones

Due to their various biological activities especially as antiasthmatic agents with dual activities of thromboxane A2 (TXA2) synthetase inhibition and bronchodialation,[12] 4-substituted 2H-phthalazin-1-ones attracted particular attention during the year 1999 and before. The AlCl$_3$-induced C-C bond forming reaction between 1,4-dichlorophthalazine (**7**) and various (hetero)arenes followed by hydrolysis of the resulting 4-substituted 1-chlorophthalazines (**8**) allowed to afford the desired 4-(hetero)aryl-2H-phthalazin-1-one derivatives (**9**) (Scheme 4).[13a] The variation of the C-4 substituent of the phthalazinone ring was the key highlight of this effort as this substituent was believed to have its crucial role in biological activities.[12] This methodology was also used as a key step by Carreira *et al.* for the preparation of a new class of biaryl P,N ligands (Fig 2) the utility of which was demonstrated in three different asymmetric reactions with three different metals.[13b,c] In a drug discovery effort, the researchers from Pfizer described the usage of this methodology during the preparation of some of their target 3-diazine substituted indole acetic acids.[13d] These compounds were explored for the identification of potent, selective, and orally bioavailable antagonists of CRTH2 (chemoattractant receptor homologous molecule expressed on Th2 cells) for the treatment of allergic inflammatory diseases. Recently various synthetic applications of chloro derivative like **8** has been reported for the access of a range of biologically significant 4-aryl/heteroaryl/alkynyl phthalazinones.[13e]

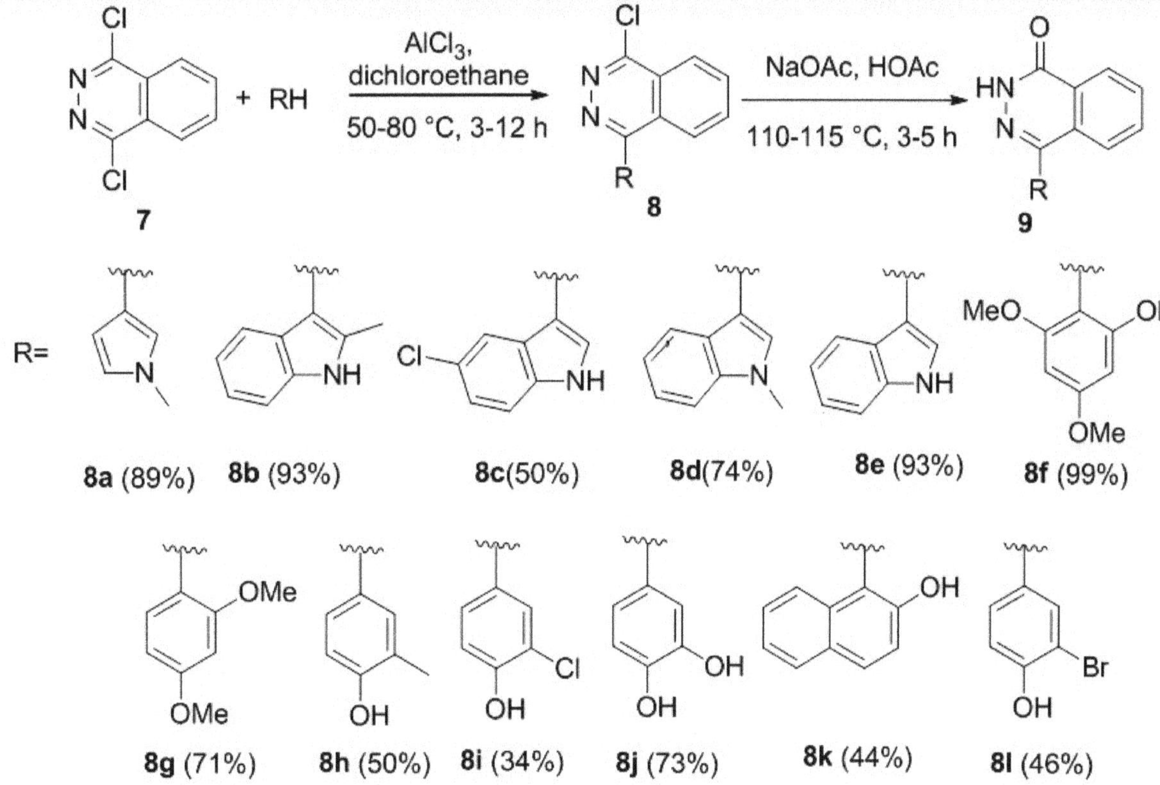

Scheme 4. Synthesis of 4-(hetero)aryl-2H-phthalazin-1-ones.

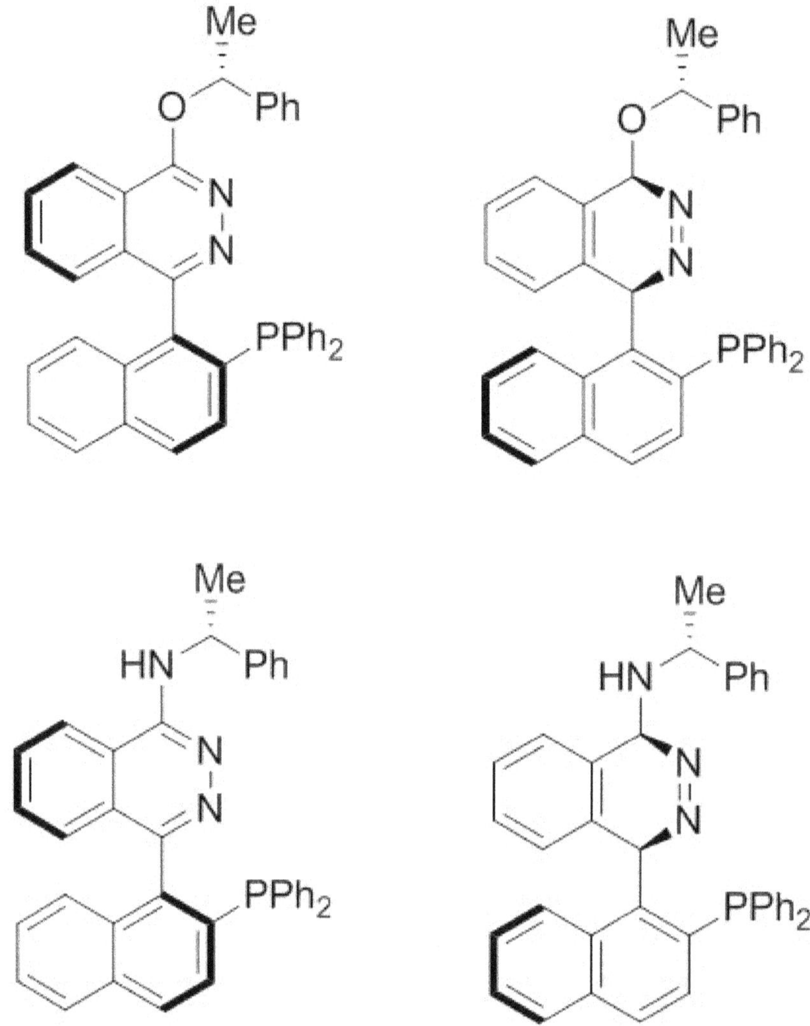

Fig. 2. Biaryl P,N ligands for Asymmetric catalysis.

CHAPTER VII

Synthesis of 2–Substituted Pyridines

A similar strategy was adopted for the synthesis of 2-aryl/heteroaryl substituted pyridine derivatives (**11**) that involved the reaction of 2-chloropyridine derivatives (**10**) with various arenes / heteroarenes in the presence of AlCl$_3$ (Scheme 5).[14a] Unlike FC reaction the use of indole was successful in this case without having any *N*-protection. This strategy was useful for generating pyridine based small molecules of biological interest.[14b] Later a nickel catalyst was identified as an efficient catalyst for this type of transformation.[15] Thus various functionalized 2-arylpyridines are obtained from 2-halopyridines in moderate to excellent yields by a one-step chemical procedure using manganese powder as reducing reagent in combination with NiBr$_2$Bpy catalyst.

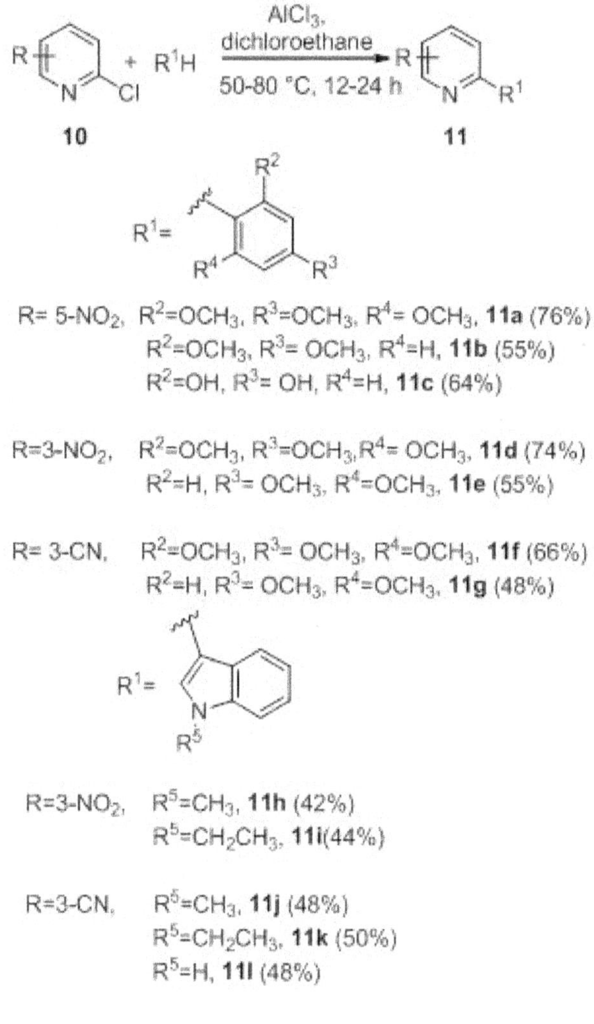

R= 5-NO$_2$, R^2=OCH$_3$, R^3=OCH$_3$, R^4= OCH$_3$, **11a** (76%)
R^2=OCH$_3$, R^3= OCH$_3$, R^4=H, **11b** (55%)
R^2=OH, R^3= OH, R^4=H, **11c** (64%)

R=3-NO$_2$, R^2=OCH$_3$, R^3=OCH$_3$, R^4= OCH$_3$, **11d** (74%)
R^2=H, R^3= OCH$_3$, R^4=OCH$_3$, **11e** (55%)

R= 3-CN, R^2=OCH$_3$, R^3= OCH$_3$, R^4=OCH$_3$, **11f** (66%)
R^2=H, R^3= OCH$_3$, R^4=OCH$_3$, **11g** (48%)

R=3-NO$_2$, R^5=CH$_3$, **11h** (42%)
R^5=CH$_2$CH$_3$, **11i** (44%)

R=3-CN, R^5=CH$_3$, **11j** (48%)
R^5=CH$_2$CH$_3$, **11k** (50%)
R^5=H, **11l** (48%)

Scheme 5. Synthesis of 2-aryl/heteroaryl substituted pyridines.

CHAPTER VIII

Synthesis of 7-(hetero)aryl-substituted pyrazolo[1,5-a]pyrimidines

Till this stage it was evident that the strategy involving the construction of a C–C bond via exploiting the reactivity of a chloro group attached to the azomethine carbon [e.g., =C–C(Cl)=N–] in the presence of AlCl$_3$ was successful. However, the reactivity of a chloride containing the –C(Cl)=C–C=N– moiety towards an AlCl$_3$-induced C–C bond forming reaction was not known until the report of 2009.[16] Thus the reaction of 7-chloro pyrazolo[1,5-a]pyrimidine (**12**) with a variety of commercially available arenes / heteroarenes in the presence of AlCl$_3$ was examined that afforded the corresponding 7-(hetero)aryl substituted pyrazolo[1,5-a]pyrimidines (**13**) successfully (Scheme 6). The reaction proceeded via the complexation of AlCl$_3$ with the nitrogen of the –C(Cl)=C–C=N– moiety to activate the chloro group thereby facilitating a nucleophilic attack by arenes or heteroarenes at the chlorine bearing carbon atom.[16]

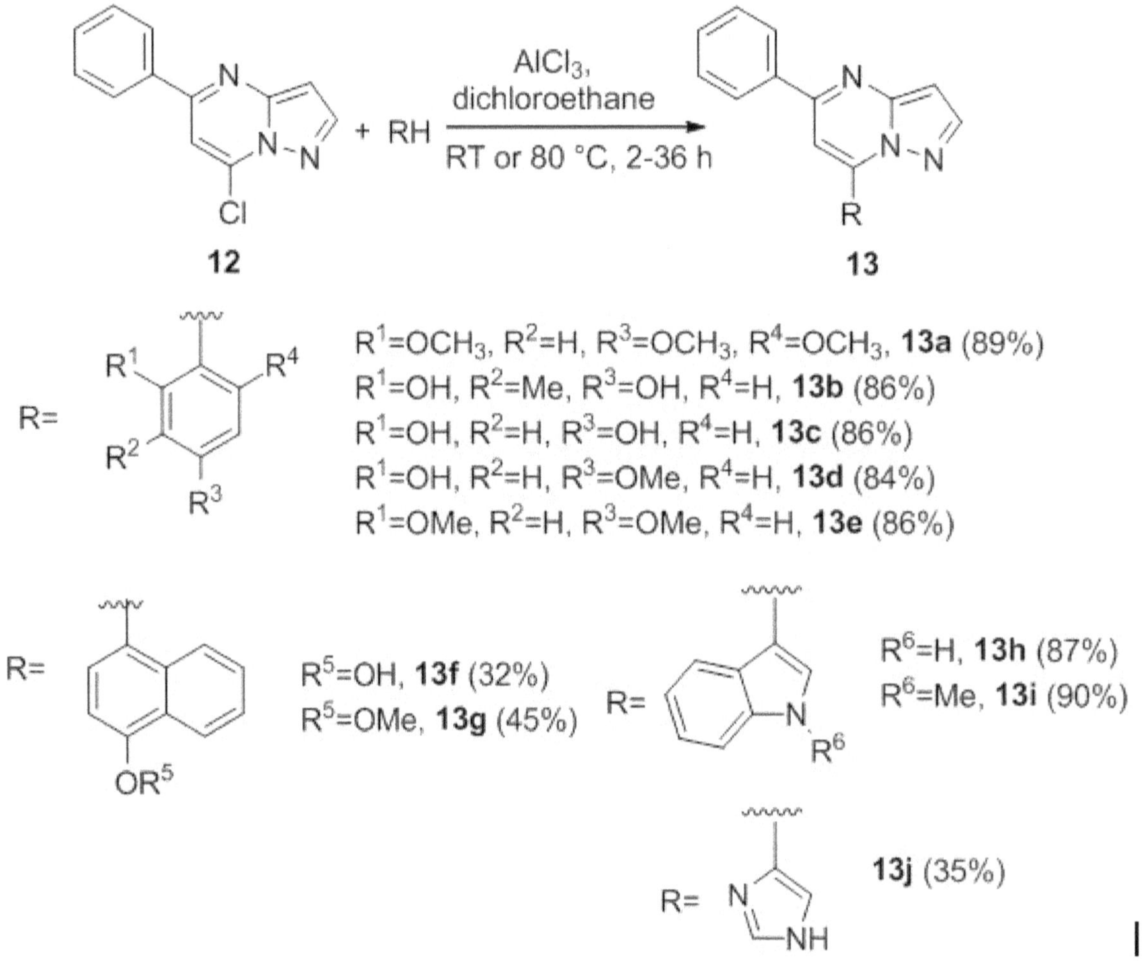

Scheme 6. Synthesis of 7-(hetero)aryl substituted pyrazolo[1,5-a]pyrimidines

CHAPTER IX

Synthesis of 2-(hetero)aryl-substituted pyrazines

In the same year *i.e.* 2009 a new synthesis of 2-(hetero)aryl substituted pyrazines (**15**) was reported using the $AlCl_3$ mediated C-C bond forming reaction between 2-chloropyrazine (**14**) and various arenes/ heteroarenes (Scheme 7).[17]

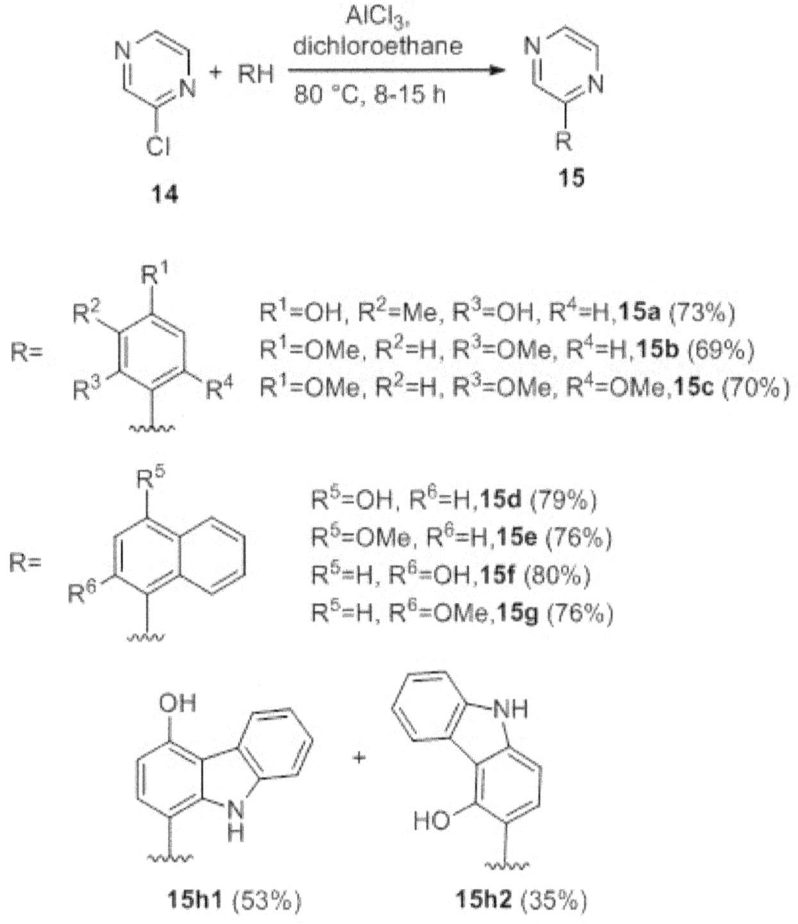

Scheme 7. Synthesis of 2-(hetero)aryl-substituted pyrazines

CHAPTER X

Synthesis of 4-(hetero)arylquinazolines/quinolines

Prompted by the report on the AlCl$_3$ mediated synthesis of 4-substituted 1-chlorophthalazines[13a] (Scheme 4), a similar strategy was adopted for the exclusive synthesis of 4-aryl / heteroarylquinazolines (**17**) and 4-aryl / heteroarylquinolines (**19**).[18a] Thus anhydrous AlCl$_3$-mediated heteroarylation of various arenes and heteroarenes with 2,4-dichloro-quinazoline (**16**) (Scheme 8) and 4-chloroquinoline (**18**) (Scheme 9) afforded the corresponding products, respectively. In a separate Med Chem effort some of the 4-(hetero)aryl quinazolines (**17**) were converted to a new class of 4-(hetero)aryl-2-piperazino quinazolines that were assessed for in vitro activity against extracellular promastigotes and intracellular amastigotes of Leishmania donovani.[18b] These compounds were also tested for anti-proliferation activity in a panel of mammalian cell lines. Couple of these compounds appeared to be interesting either in anti-leishmanial assay or anti-proliferative assay.

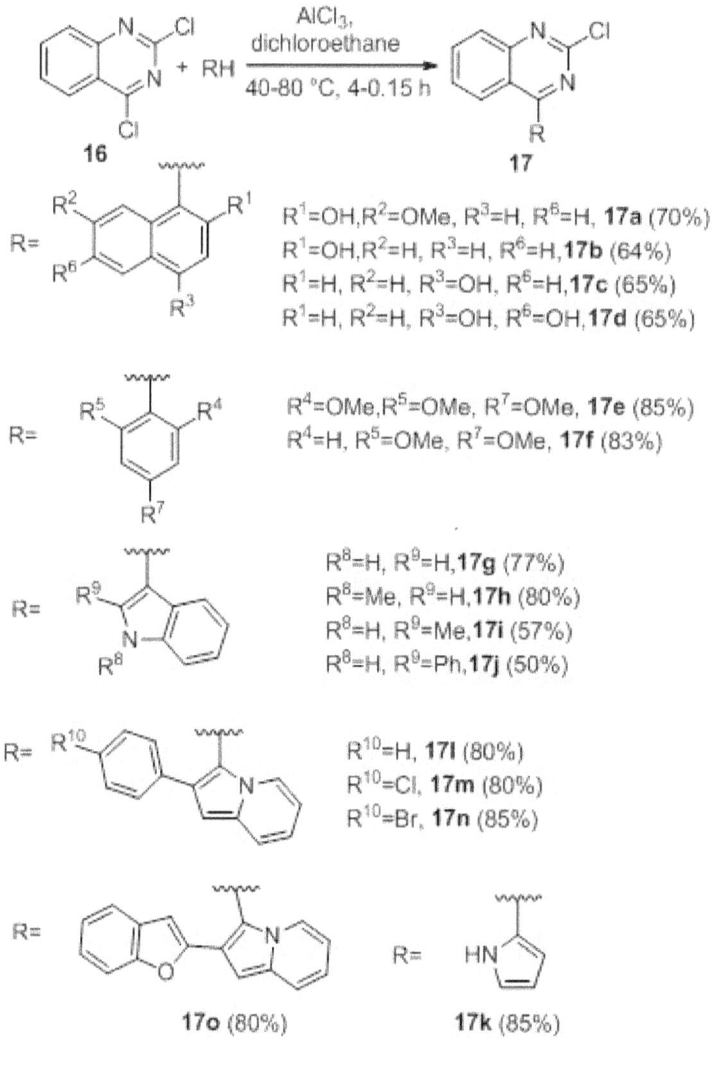

Scheme 8. Regioselective synthesis of 4-(hetero)arylquinazolines.

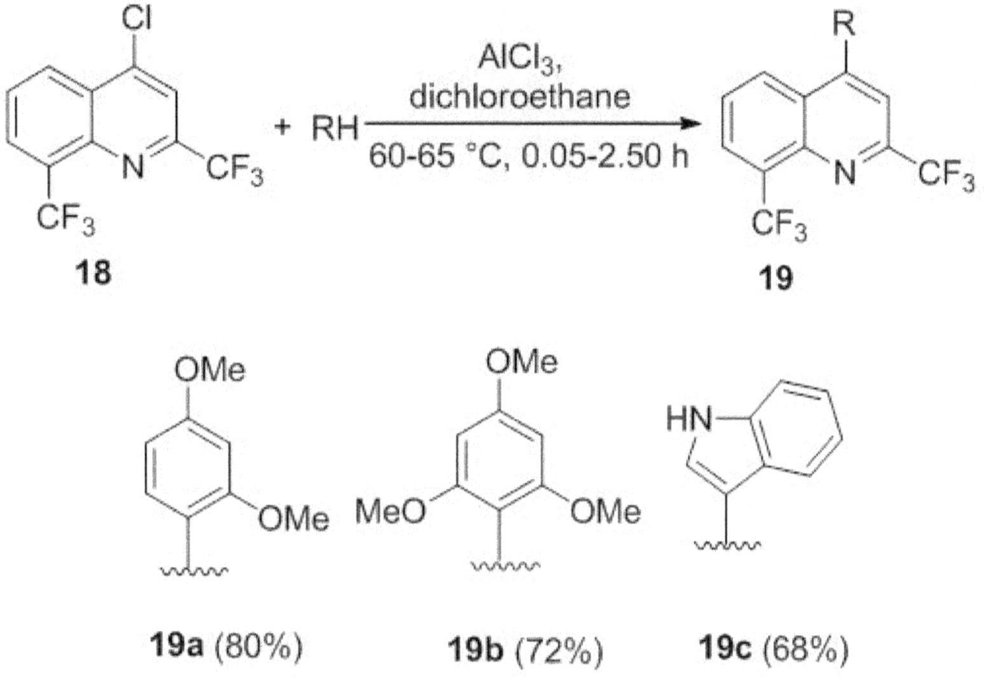

Scheme 9. $AlCl_3$-mediated synthesis of 4-(hetero)arylquinolines

The use of 2-(hetero)aryl 4-chloro quinazoline (**17**) in $AlCl_3$ mediated heteroarylation reaction was also successful and afforded the corresponding 4-aryl substituted products (**20**) (Scheme 10) of potential biological interest.[18c] Notably, the use of $InCl_3$ under microwave irradiation (in a pressure-tight microwave tube generally at ~ 120 °C) was found to be effective for the similar C-C bond forming reactions of several p-deficient heterocyclic substrates including quinolines and quinazolines.[19] The generality of this method was exemplified by a large number of various examples.

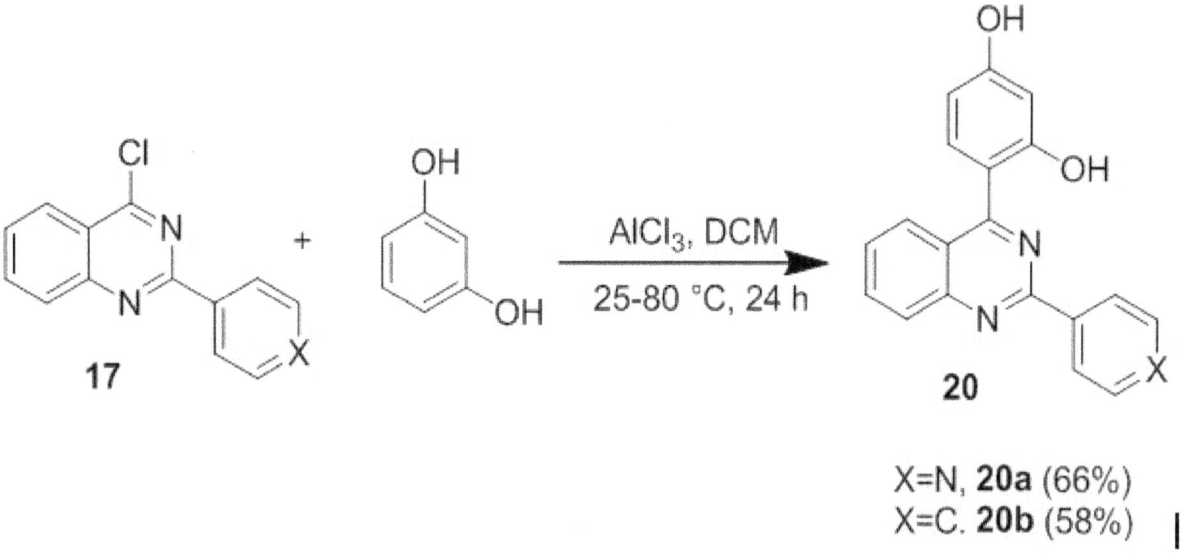

Scheme 10. Synthesis of 4-aryl substituted 2-(hetero)arylquinazolines.

CHAPTER XI

Synthesis of 4–aryl substituted pyrazolopyrimidines

In a drug discovery program a library of small molecules based on new bicyclo heterocyclic framework was necessary for the identification of agents to treat a variety of conditions and disease states associated with, for example, cellular proliferation, infammation, glycosidase expression, or the low expression of perlecan. With this goal some pyrazolopyrimidines were prepared by using the $AlCl_3$ mediated heteroarylation method.[20] Thus 4-chloro pyrazolopyrimidines (**21**) were treated with phenols in the presence of $AlCl_3$ to give the desired products (**22**) *via* a C-C bond forming reaction (Scheme 11). These compounds were tested for their activity separately in MCP-1, VCAM-1 and IL-6 enzyme-linked immunosorbent assay.

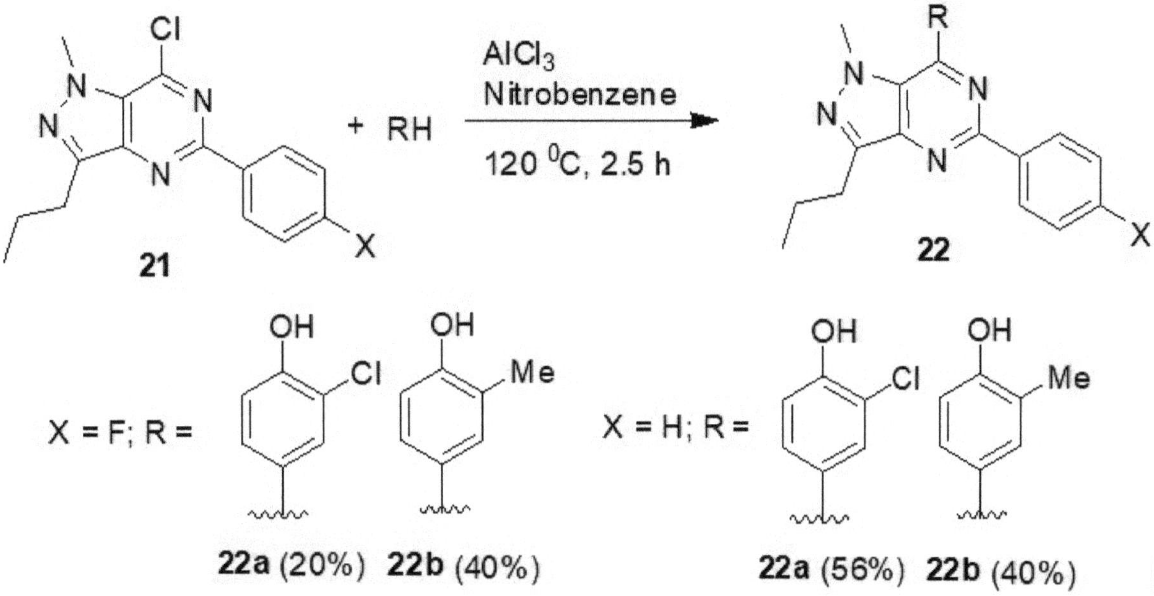

Scheme 11. Synthesis of 4-substituted pyrazolo pyrimidins.

CHAPTER XII

Synthesis of 4-(hetero)aryl substituted thienopyrimidines

In view of remarkable affinity and selectivity of thieno[2,3-*d*]pyrimidine derivatives for the 5-HT3 receptor[21] a new template based on this framework was designed having three positions for the introduction of diversity (the C-4 position being an important one of them). Accordingly, a series of 4-(hetero)aryl substituted thieno[2,3-*d*]pyrimidines (**24**) were prepared *via* the reaction of 4-chloro thieno[2,3-*d*]pyrimidine (**23**) with various commercially available arenes / heteroarenes in the presence of AlCl₃ (Scheme 12).[22] Notably, this is one of the few examples (after Scheme 10 and 11) of using a –C(Cl)=N–C=N– moiety in AlCl₃ mediated C-C bond forming reaction after the successful use of =C–C(Cl)=N– and –C(Cl)=C–C=N– moiety as presented in earlier sections.

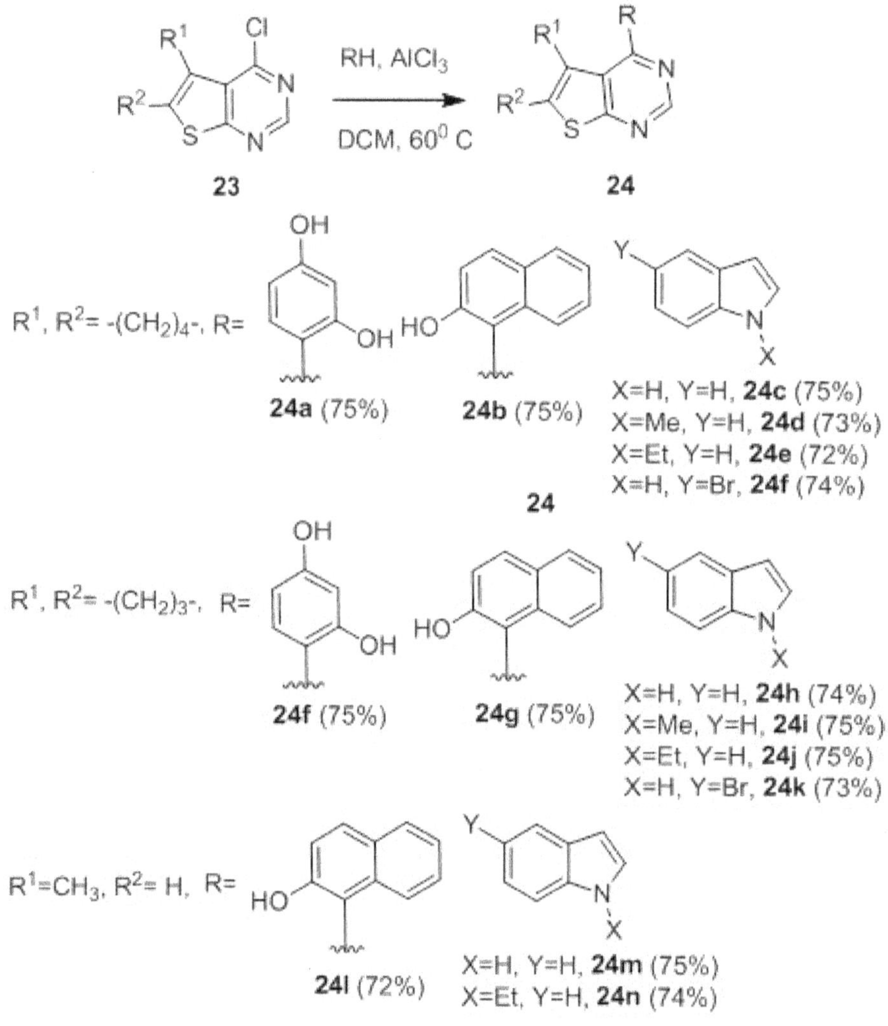

Scheme 12. Synthesis of 4-(hetero)aryl substituted thienopyrimidines

CHAPTER XIII

Synthesis of 6-(hetero)aryl purines

While studies on biological activities of 6-arylpurines were performed using easily available purines bearing simple aryl groups, the analogues bearing highly substituted and/or functionalized aryl moieties remain to be explored until 2010. Moreover, 6-arylpurine bases and their nucleosides were of particular importance due to anti-HCV, cytostatic, and antimycobacterial activities.[23] Thus highly functionalized C6-aryl-substituted purine analogues (**26**) were synthesized *via* direct arylation of 6-chloropurine (**25**) with arenes / heteroarenes promoted by anhydrous AlCl₃ in a single step (Scheme 13).[24] The reaction was completed within 30 min and afforded a range of desired products.

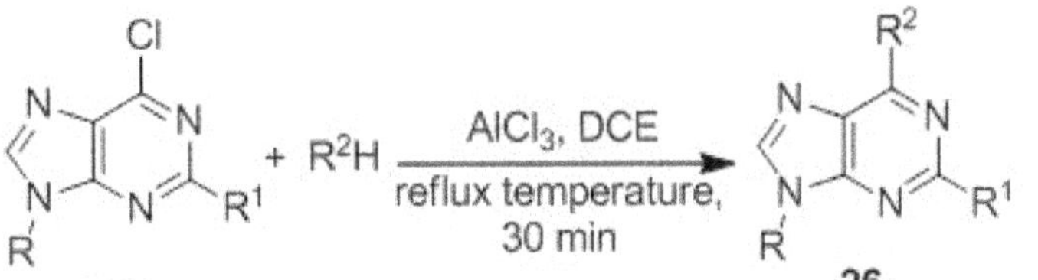

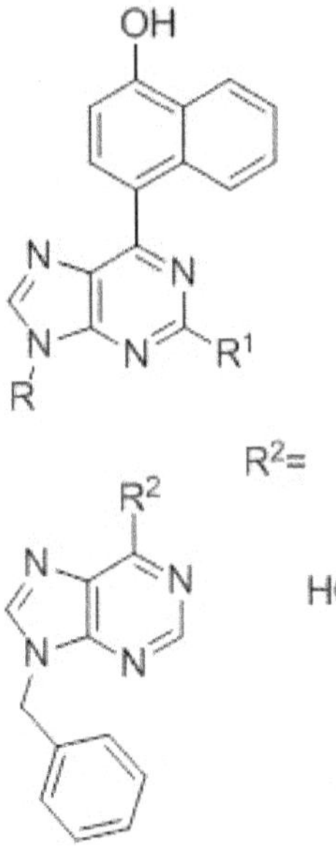

26a: R=-CH₂-C₆H₅, R¹=H (75%); **26b**: R=-CH₂-C₆H₅-Cl(O), R¹=H (76%): **26c**: R=-CH₂-CH₂=CH₂, R¹=H (70%); **26d**: R=H, R¹=H (53%); **26e**: R=-CH₂-C₆H₅, R¹=Cl (85%); **26f**: R=-CH₂-C₆H₅-Cl(O), R¹=Cl (87%); **26g**: R=-CH₂-CH₂=CH₂, R¹=Cl (74%); **26h**: R=-CH₂-(CH₂)₂-CH₃, R¹=Cl (75%); **26i**: R=H, R¹=Cl (75%); **26j**: R=R=-CH₂-(CH₂)₂-CH₃, R¹=NH₂ (92%)

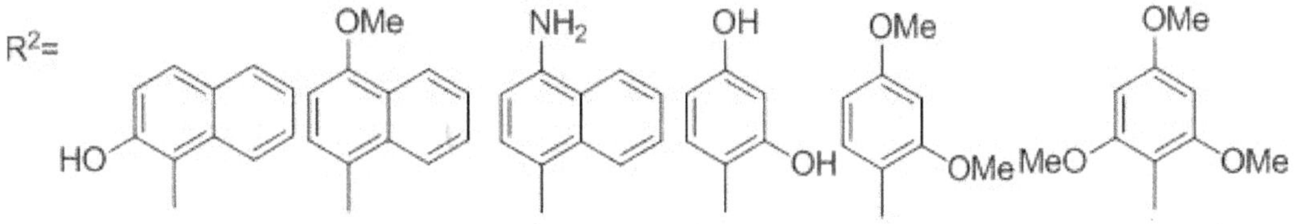

26k (76%) **26l** (85%) **26m** (25%) **26n** (51%) **26o** (85%) **26p** (95%)

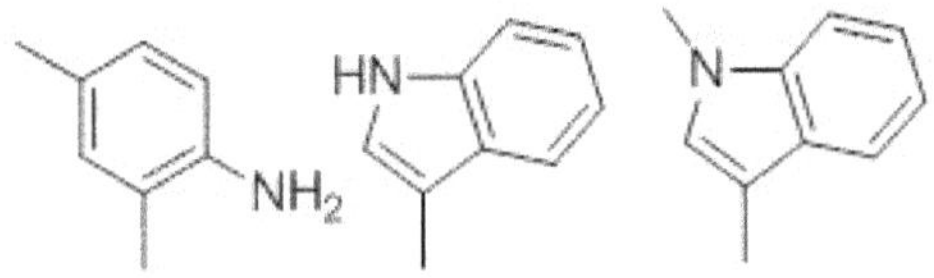

26q (40%) **26r** (87%) **26s** (90%)

Scheme 13. Synthesis of 6-(hetero)aryl purines

CHAPTER XIV

Synthesis of 2-(1H-indol-3-yl)quinoline-3-carbonitrile derivatives

Based on literature report on PDE4 (phosphodiesterase 4) inhibitory properties of indoles[25a] as well as quinolines[25b,c] and the possible role of the cyano group in pharmacological activities a new scaffold was designed by attaching a cyano group at an appropriate position of the 2-indolyl quinoline framework. Subsequently, a series of 2-(1H-indol-3-yl)quinoline-3-carbonitriles (**28**) were synthesized and evaluated *in vitro* as potential inhibitors of PDE4B.[26] Notable, PDE4 inhibitors are known to be useful for the treatment of inflammatory and immunological diseases including asthma and chronic obstructive pulmonary disease (COPD).[25d] The AlCl$_3$-mediated C–C bond forming reaction between 2-chloroquinoline-3-carbonitrile (**27**) and various indoles was used to synthesize the target compounds (**28**) (Scheme 14) many of which showed PDE4 inhibitory properties *in vitro*.[26] A brief structure–activity relationship (SAR) studies within the series along with docking studies of a representative compound (EC$_{50}$ ~0.89 µM) was performed.

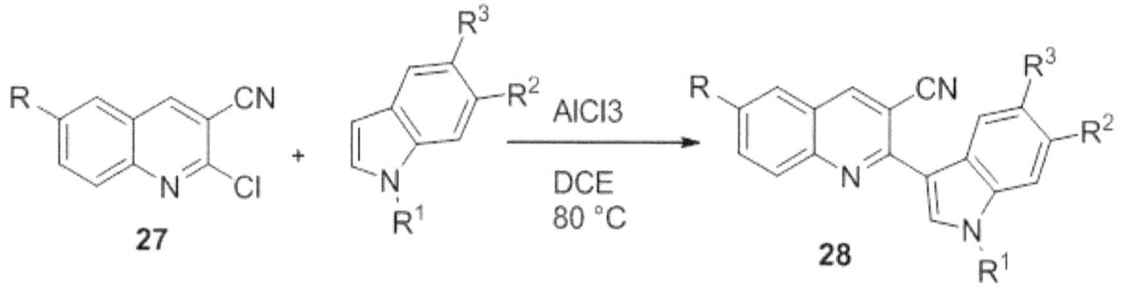

28a:R=H (88%), R^1=H, R^2=H, R^3=H (85%); **28b**:R=H, R^1=CH$_3$, R^2=H, R^3=H (80%);
28c:R=H, R^1=CH$_3$, R^2=H, R^3=Cl (80%); **28d**:R=H, R^1=CH$_3$, R^2=H, R^3=Br (80%);
28e:R=H, R^1=CH$_3$, R^2=F, R^3=F (80%); **28f**:R=H, R^1=OCH$_3$, R^2=F, R^3=OCH$_3$ (75%);
28g:R=H, R^1=CH$_3$, R^2=OCH$_3$, R^3=H (72%); **28h**:R=CH$_3$, R^1=H, R^2=H, R^3=H (85%);
28i:R=CH$_3$, R^1=H, R^2=H, R^3=Cl (81%); **28j**:R=CH$_3$, R^1=H, R^2=H, R^3=Br (80%);
28k:R=CH$_3$, R^1=H, R^2=H, R^3=OCH$_3$ (75%); **28l**:R=CH$_3$, R^1=H, R^2=OCH$_3$, R^3=H
78%);

Scheme 14. Synthesis of 2-(1H-indol-3-yl)quinoline derivatives.

CHAPTER XV

Synthesis of mono and 2,3-disubstituted quinoxalines

The reported antibacterial properties of quinoxaline[27a] and indole derivatives[27b,c] prompted researchers to design a new template by combining the structural features of these heterocycles in a single molecular entity. This template was thought to be useful for the identification and development of promising antibacterial agents. Accordingly, $AlCl_3$ induced (hetero)arylation of 2,3-dichloroquinoxaline (**29**) was used to afford mono and 2,3-disubstituted quinoxalines (including the symmetrical and unsymmetrical analogues) (**30** and **31**, Scheme 15 and 16).[28] Some of the compounds synthesized were tested for chorismate mutase (CM) inhibitory properties *in vitro* and one compound showed promising activity representing one of the few examples of chorismate mutase inhibition by a heteroarene based small molecule. It is mention worthy that CM, an enzyme that catalyzes the conversion of chorismate to prephenate in the shikimate pathway[29a] for the biosynthesis of aromatic amino acids is considered as a novel target for the identification of effective antibacterial agents.[29b] The 2,3-disubstituted quinoxaline derivatives has also been explored as antileishmanial and antitrypanosomal agents.[29c]

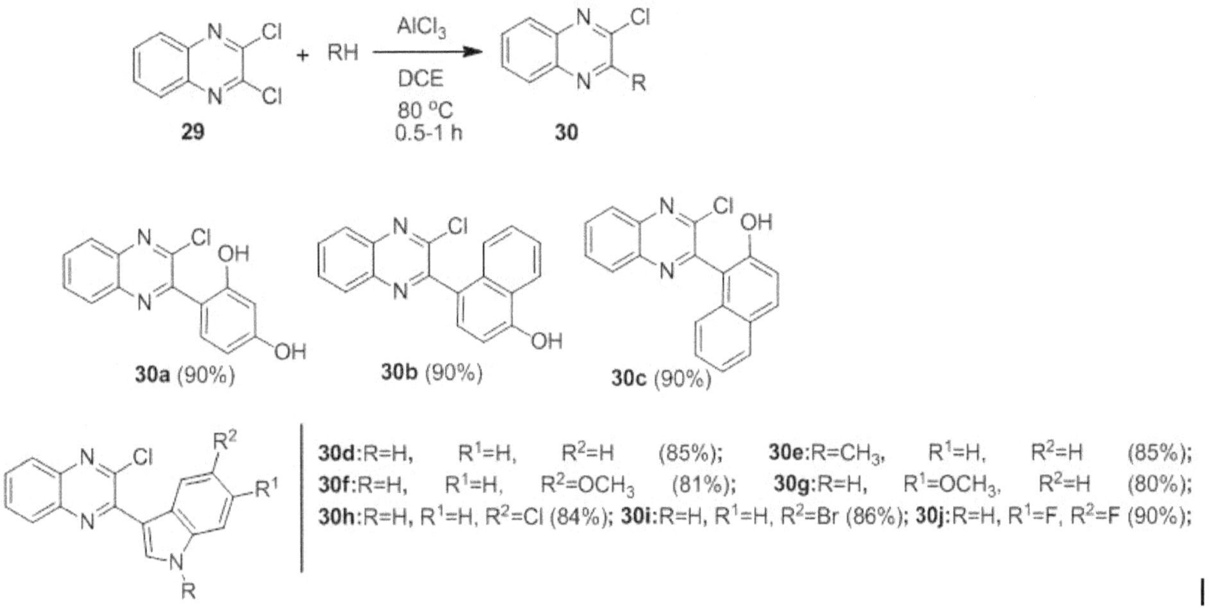

AlCl3
+ RH
DCE
80 °C
0.5-1 h
29
30
30a (90%)
30b (90%)
30c (90%)
30d:R=H, R1=H, R2=H (85%); 30e:R=CH3, R1=H, R2=H (85%);
30f:R=H, R1=H, R2=OCH3 (81%); 30g:R=H, R1=OCH3, R2=H (80%);
30h:R=H, R1=H, R2=Cl (84%); 30i:R=H, R1=H, R2=Br (86%); 30j:R=H, R1=F, R2=F (90%);

Scheme 15. Synthesis of 2-(hetero)aryl substituted 3-chloroquinoxaline

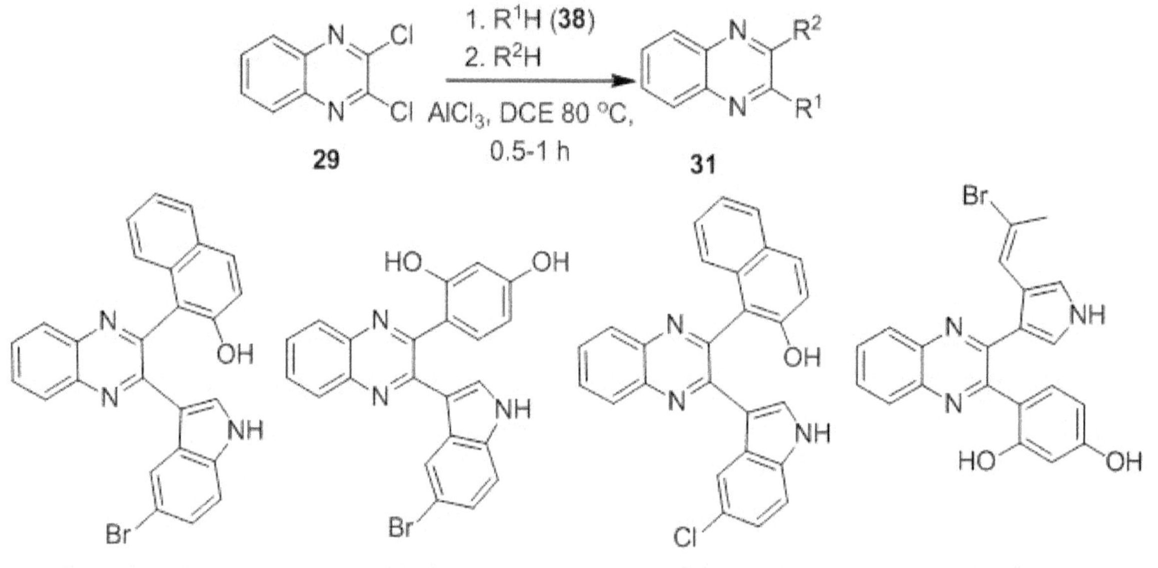

31a (90%) **31b** (90%) **31c** (90%) **31d** (81%)

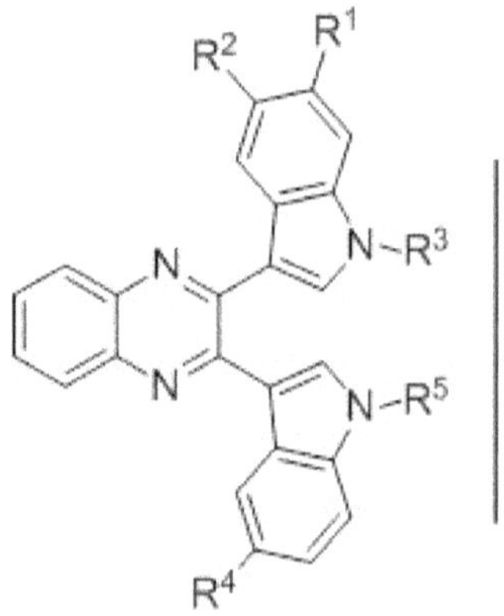

31e: $R^1=OCH_3$: $R^2=H$: $R^3=H$: $R^4=H$: $R^5=H$ (78%); **31f**: $R^1=H$: $R^2=H$: $R^3=H$: $R^4=Br$: $R^5=H$ (80%): **31g**: $R^1=H$: $R^2=H$: $R^3=CH_3$: $R^4=Br$: $R^5=H$ (80%); **31h**: $R^1=F$: $R^2=F$: $R^3=CH_3$: $R^4=Br$: $R^5=H$ (80%); **31h**: $R^1=H$: $R^2=H$: $R^3=CH_3$: $R^4=H$: $R^5=CH_3$ (88%); **31h**: $R^1=H$: $R^2=F$: $R^3=H$: $R^4=H$: $R^5=H$ (90%)

Scheme 16. Synthesis of symmetrical and unsymmetrical 2,3-disubstituted quinoxaline

CHAPTER XVI

Heteroarylation–coupling–cyclization: sequential approach

While the heteroarylation method was established as an effective strategy for the synthesis of certain class of *N*-heteroarenes its application for the synthesis of relatively more complex compounds was desirable. In other words it was necessary to assess the applicability and scope of heteroarylation strategy further. Some of these efforts are presented in the following sections.

CHAPTER XVII

Synthesis of 6-substituted chromenoquinoxalines

The ability of $AlCl_3$ induced heteroarylation to install a phenol moiety on an *N*-heterocyclic ring allowed researcher taking advantage of this acidic OH group in a subsequent reaction. For example, it was envisaged that a phenolic OH present at the δ-position to the alkynyl moiety might undergo an intramolecular cyclization in a regioselective manner. With this thought effort was devoted to develop a two-step protocol for the regioselective construction of a fused 2-ylidene chromene ring. This was finally achieved by using $AlCl_3$-induced C–C bond formation followed by Pd/C–Cu mediate coupling-cyclization method (Scheme 17). A number of chromeno[4,3-*b*]quinoxaline derivatives (**33**) were prepared from 2,3-dichloroquinoxaline (**29**) *via* **32** by using this strategy.[30] Notably, the coupling-cyclization occurred in a single pot via a Sonogashira-type alkynylation of **32** in the same pot. The X-ray diffraction study of a representative chromeno[4,3-*b*]quinoxaline derivative confirmed the presence of an exocyclic C–C double bond with Z-geometry. Some of these compounds showed good activity against leukemia cell lines whereas others were found to be effective against breast cancer cell lines.

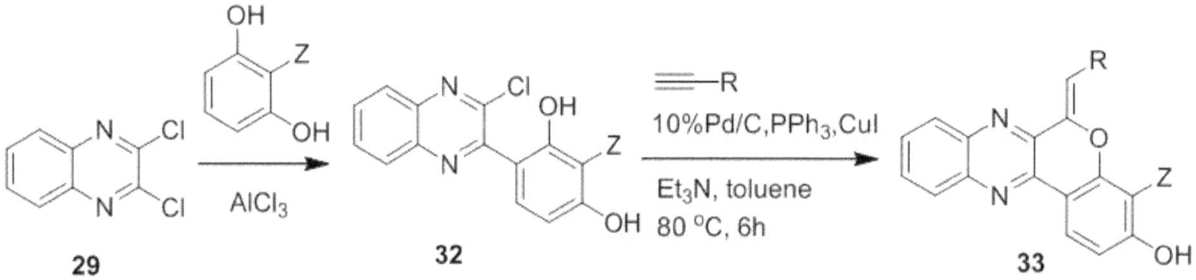

33a: Z=H:R=Ph (82%); **33b**: Z=H:R=$C_6H_4CH_3$-*p* (80%);**33c**: Z=H:R=-$(CH_2)_3CN$ (80%);**33d**: Z=CH_3:R=$C_6H_4CH_3$-*p* (80%);**33e**: Z=CH_3:R=-$(CH_2)_3CN$ (78)%; **33f**: Z=CH_3:R=-$C(CH_3)_3$ (80%);**33g**: Z=CH_3:R=-$Si(CH_3)_3$ (82%);**33h**: Z=CH_3:R=-CMe_2OH (80%);**33i**: Z=CH_3:R=$(CH_2)_3Me$ (78%);**33j**: Z=CH_3:R=$(CH_2)_4Me$ (80%);**33k**: Z=CH_3:R=$(CH_2)_5Me$(80%)

Scheme-17. Synthesis of 6-substituted 6*H*-chromeno[4,3-*b*]quinoxalin-3-ol

CHAPTER XVIII

Synthesis of indolophenazines

In view of the known human NAD(P)H quinoneoxido reductase (NQO1) inhibitory properties of a indolophenazine derivative[31] a series of indolophenazine derivatives were synthesized and evaluated for their anticancer activities. Thus TFA-mediated cyclization of 3-alkynyl substituted 2-(indol-3-yl)quinoxalines (**36**) that proceeded *via* an intramolecular hydroarylation (IMHA) of alkynes afforded the target compounds (**37**) (Scheme 18) as new and potential cytotoxic agents.[32] The starting compounds were prepared via a two step method e.g. the reaction of 2,3-dichloroquinoxaline (**34**) with various indoles in the presence of $AlCl_3$ followed by Pd/C-catalyzed coupling of the resulting 2-chloro-3-(indol-3-yl)quinoxaline derivatives (**35**) with a variety of terminal alkynes. Thus $AlCl_3$ mediated method allowed development of an operationally simple and straightforward method for a new and easy access to indolophenazines.

Three of these compounds showed cytotoxic properties when tested against two cancer cell lines.

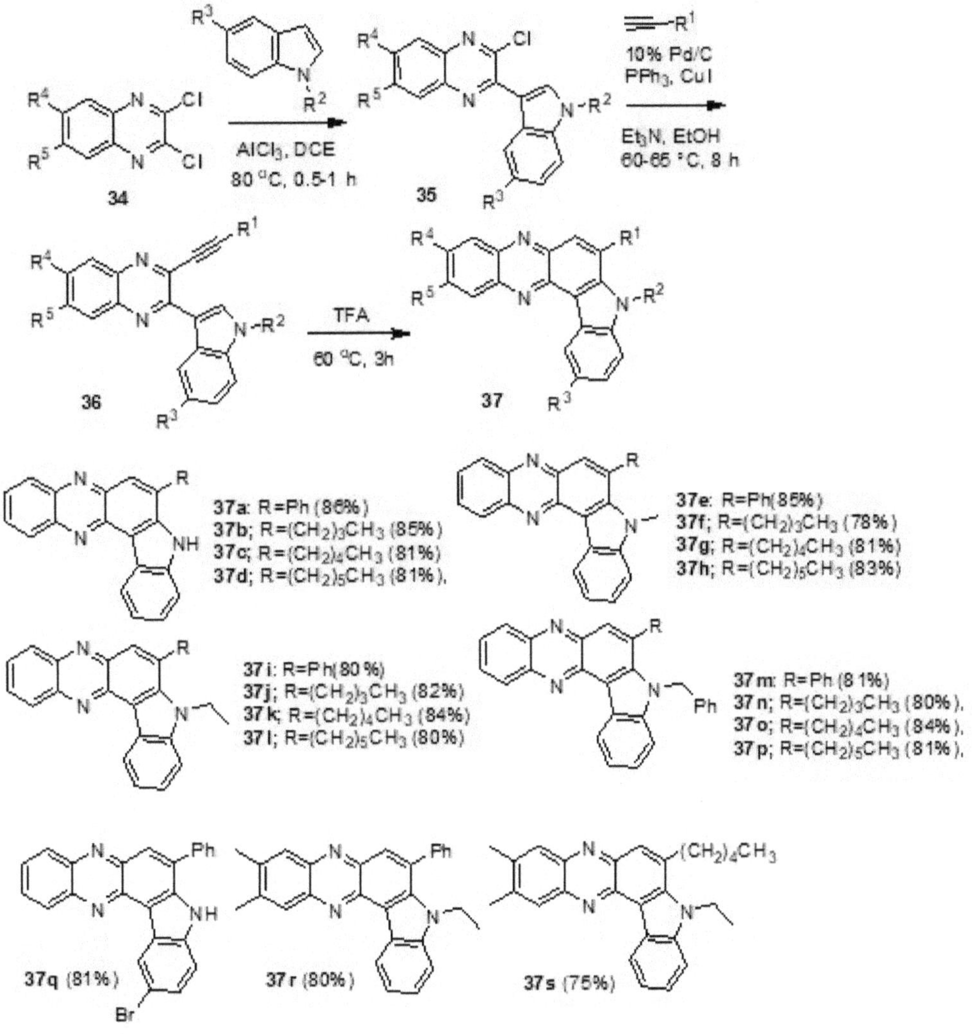

Scheme 18. Synthesis of 8*H*-indolo[3,2-*a*]phenazine derivatives.

CHAPTER XIX

Heterocyclization–cyclization in a single pot

24

The multi-step approach where AlCl₃ induced heteroarylation was a key step appeared to be interesting as presented in the previous sections. However, it was observed that apart from participating in the heteroarylation step AlCl₃ was also able to facilitate further chemical transformations in the same pot. Two such examples that afforded compounds of potential pharmacological significance are presented below.

CHAPTER XX

Synthesis of benzofuran fused N-heterocycles

With the goal of evaluating their PDE4 inhibitory properties a series of nitrogen containing heterocycles possessing benzofuran moiety as a central ring was designed. One-pot synthesis of these benzofuran fused *N*-heterocycles (**39**) was accomplished *via* $AlCl_3$-mediated C–C followed by C–O bond formation between 2,3-dichloropyrazine or its derivatives (**38**) and phenols (Scheme 19).[33] After assessing the PDE4 inhibition *in vitro* the docking study was also performed using the best active compound.

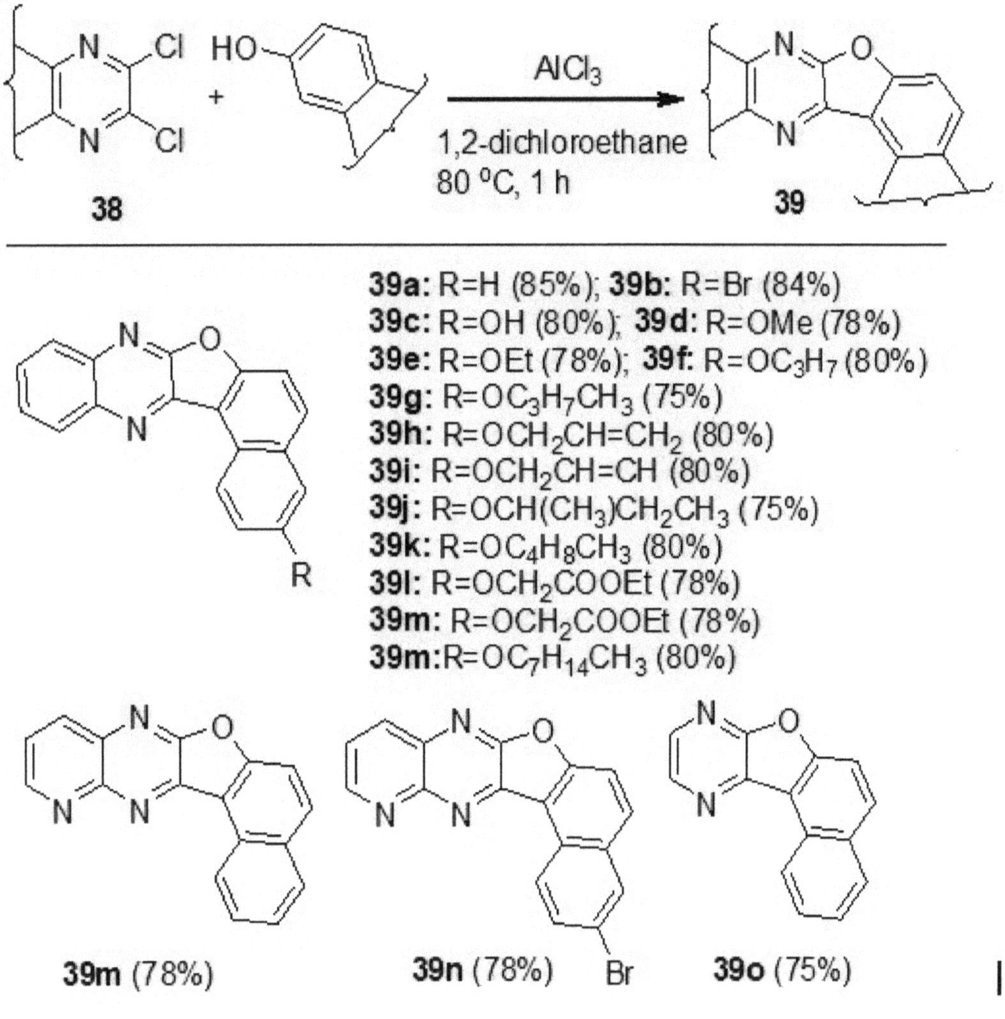

39a: R=H (85%); **39b:** R=Br (84%)
39c: R=OH (80%); **39d:** R=OMe (78%)
39e: R=OEt (78%); **39f:** R=OC_3H_7 (80%)
39g: R=$OC_3H_7CH_3$ (75%)
39h: R=$OCH_2CH=CH_2$ (80%)
39i: R=$OCH_2CH=CH$ (80%)
39j: R=$OCH(CH_3)CH_2CH_3$ (75%)
39k: R=$OC_4H_8CH_3$ (80%)
39l: R=OCH_2COOEt (78%)
39m: R=OCH_2COOEt (78%)
39m: R=$OC_7H_{14}CH_3$ (80%)

39m (78%) **39n** (78%) Br **39o** (75%)

Scheme 19. Synthesis of benzofuran fused *N*-heterocycles.

CHAPTER XXI

Synthesis of pyrano[3,4-b]indole fused quinoxalines

The pyrano[3,4-*b*]indole framework is a central part of Lamellarin D (Fig. 1),[34] a potent inhibitor of topoisomerase I that showed strong cytotoxic activity against tumor cell lines. It was hypothesized that combination of the structural features of pyrano[3,4-*b*]indole (the central core of Lamellarin D) and quinoxaline in a single molecular entity might be useful for the design of potential anticancer agents. Accordingly, a number of pyrano[3,4-*b*]indole fused quinoxalines (**41**) were synthesized from 2,3-dichloroquinoxalines (**40**) via a one-pot AlCl$_3$-mediated heteroarylation-cyclization method that involved the construction of the central pyranone ring (Scheme 20).[35] Several of these compounds showed promising growth inhibition of cervical and lung cancer cells and good interactions with topoisomerase I in silico.

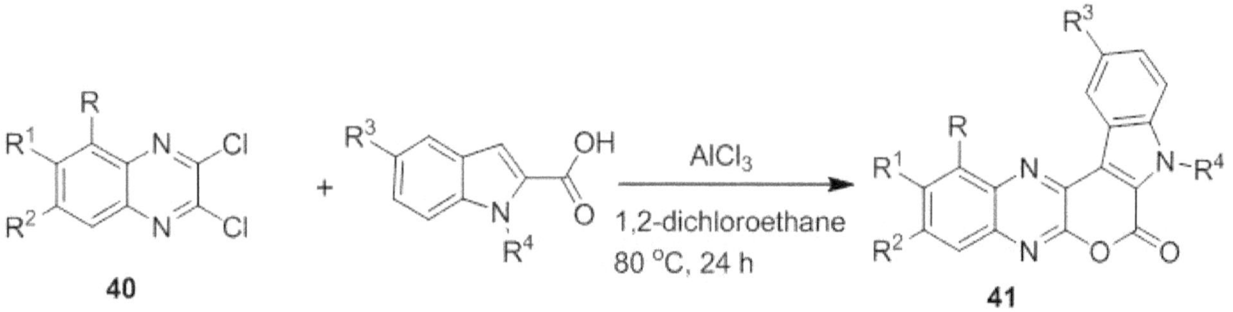

41a: R=H: R^1=H: R^2=H:R^3=H:R^4=H (85%); **41b**: R=H: R^1=H: R^2=H:R^3=H:R^4=CH$_3$ (76%); **41c** R=H: R^1=H: R^2=H:R^3=H:R^4=CH$_2$CH$_3$ (85%); **41d**: R=H: R^1=H: R^2=H:R^3=H:R^4=CH$_2$CH=CH (75%); **41e**: R=H: R^1=H: R^2=H:R^3=F:R^4=H (68%); **41f**: R=H: R^1=H: R^2=H:R^3=CH$_3$:R^4=H (83%); **41g**: R=CH$_3$: R^1=H: R^2=H:R^3=H:R^4=H (82%); **41h**: R=H: R^1=CH$_3$: R^2=H:R^3=H:R^4=CH$_3$ (77%); **41i**: R=H: R^1=CH$_3$: R^2=CH$_3$:R^3=H:R^4=H (71%); **41j**: R=H: R^1=CH$_3$: R^2=CH$_3$:R^3=H:R^4=CH$_2$CH$_3$ (68%); **41k**: R=CH$_3$: R^1=H: R^2=CH$_3$:R^3=H:R^4=H (79%).

Scheme 20. Synthesis of pyrano[3,4-*b*]indole fused quinoxalines

CHAPTER XXII

The amination reaction

27

Unlike the amination of aliphatic halides, the amination of aromatic halides is known to be not a simple and straightforward process due to the lower reactivity of the later class of halides. The problem becomes more complicated when aromatic amines were used as aminating agents. Accordingly, it was observed that the preparation of *N*-aryl substituted 3-chloroquinoxalin-2-amine was an initial challenge as unlike aliphatic amines[36] the nucleophilic substitution of 2,3-dichloroquinoxaline (**29**) with aromatic amines did not proceed well. While the reaction proceeded in the presence of a base, for example, Et$_3$N a mixture of products, that is, the mono amine derivative along with the corresponding N^2,N^3-diarylquinoxaline-2,3-diamines were isolated in this case. Finally, the use of AlCl$_3$ was found to be effective in such cases. The use of this strategy in the preparation of pyrrolo[2,3-*b*]quinoxaline derivatives is presented in the following section.

CHAPTER XXIII

Synthesis of 1,3-disubstituted pyrrolo[2,3-b]quinoxalines

Based on an earlier observation that 2-substituted pyrrolo[2,3-*b*]quinoxalines[37] interact with luciferase preferentially over the enzyme PDE4B (a sub type of PDE4) 1,3-disubstituted pyrrolo[2,3-*b*]quinoxalines were designed as potential inhibitors of PDE4B. Notably, PDE4B inhibitory properties of compounds were determined in vitro by using a luciferase reporter gene assay. Nevertheless, *in silico* studies were performed to address this issue. Consequently, a series of 1,3-disubstituted pyrrolo[2,3-*b*]quinoxalines were conveniently prepared by using a ligand and phase transfer catalyst (PTC) free intramolecular Heck cyclization strategy in good yields.[38] The starting amines **42** were synthesized *via* the reaction of 2,3-dichloroquinoxalines with aromatic amines in the presence of AlCl$_3$ (Scheme 21). The amines (**42**) were then allylated to give the *N*-allyl substituted amines **43** (Scheme 22) that on intramolecular Heck cyclization afforded the desired compounds (**44**) (Scheme 21).[38] While, the strategy of AlCl$_3$ mediated C–N bond forming reaction was not known earlier the methodology however did not work when an aliphatic amine was used perhaps due to its complexation with AlCl$_3$. Some of the 2-substituted pyrrolo[2,3-*b*]quinoxalines showed significant inhibition of PDE4B (IC$_{50}$ ≈ 5–14 μM) and growth inhibition of oral cancer cells (CAL 27) but not inhibition of luciferase in vitro. They also showed acceptable safety profiles but no apoptosis in zebrafish embryos.[38]

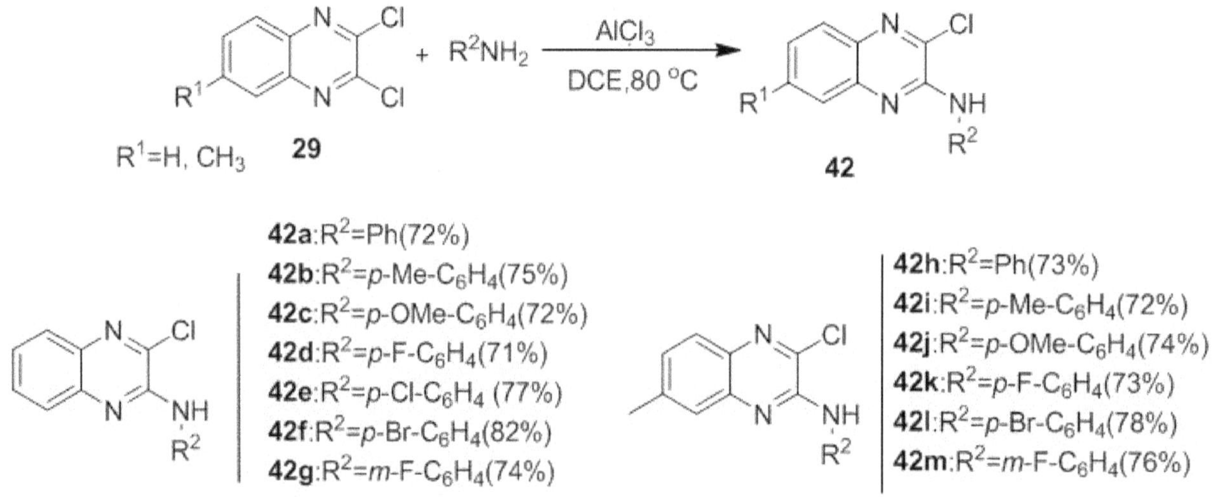

Scheme 21. Synthesis of *N*-aryl-3-chloroquinoxaline-2-amines

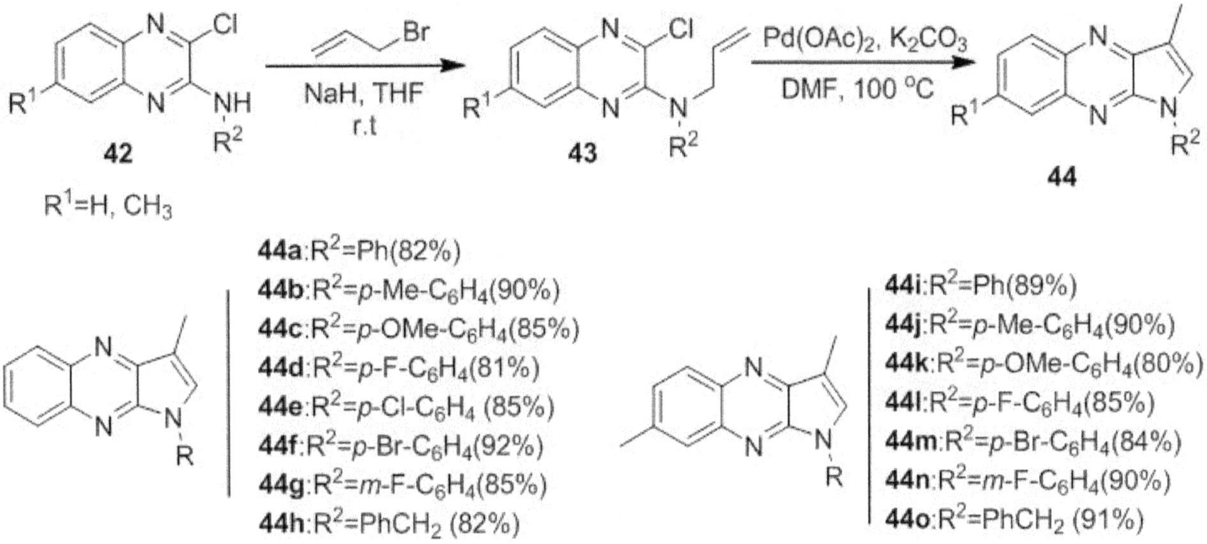
Br
NaH, THF
r.t
Pd(OAc)2, K2CO3
DMF, 100 °C
42
43
44
R1=H, CH3
44a:R2=Ph(82%)
44b:R2=p-Me-C6H4(90%)
44c:R2=p-OMe-C6H4(85%)
44d:R2=p-F-C6H4(81%)
44e:R2=p-Cl-C6H4 (85%)
44f:R2=p-Br-C6H4(92%)
44g:R2=m-F-C6H4(85%)
44h:R2=PhCH2 (82%)
44i:R2=Ph(89%)
44j:R2=p-Me-C6H4(90%)
44k:R2=p-OMe-C6H4(80%)
44l:R2=p-F-C6H4(85%)
44m:R2=p-Br-C6H4(84%)
44n:R2=m-F-C6H4(90%)
44o:R2=PhCH2 (91%)

Scheme 22. Synthesis of 1,3-disubstituted pyrrolo[2,3-*b*]quinoxalines

CHAPTER XXIV

Synthesis of 1,2-disubstituted pyrrolo[2,3-b]quinoxalines

Reports describing pyrrolo[1,2-*a*]quinoxaline derivatives as potential anticancer agents[39] prompted researchers to examine the anti cancer properties of compounds based on regioisomeric pyrrolo[2,3-*b*]quinoxaline scaffold. Thus the synthesis of a series of relevant compounds was undertaken. Initially, the strategy based on $AlCl_3$ mediated C–N bond forming reaction between 2,3-dichloroquinoxaline and anilines was used for the preparation of *N*-aryl substituted 3-chloroquinoxalin-2-amines (Scheme 21). A related *N*-benzyl derivative, however, was prepared *via* a conventional method. These *N*-alkyl/aryl substituted 3-chloroquinoxalin-2-amines (**45**) on coupling with terminal alkynes in toluene under Pd/C–Cu catalysis afforded a range of 1,2-disubstituted pyrrolo[2,3-*b*]quinoxalines (**46**) within 3–5 h in good to excellent yields (Scheme 23).[40] The reaction proceeded *via* a sequential coupling-cyclization process in the same pot. Some of the compounds synthesized showed promising anti-proliferative properties when tested *in vitro* against two cancer cell lines. Docking studies indicated that these molecules interact well with human Akt *in silico*.

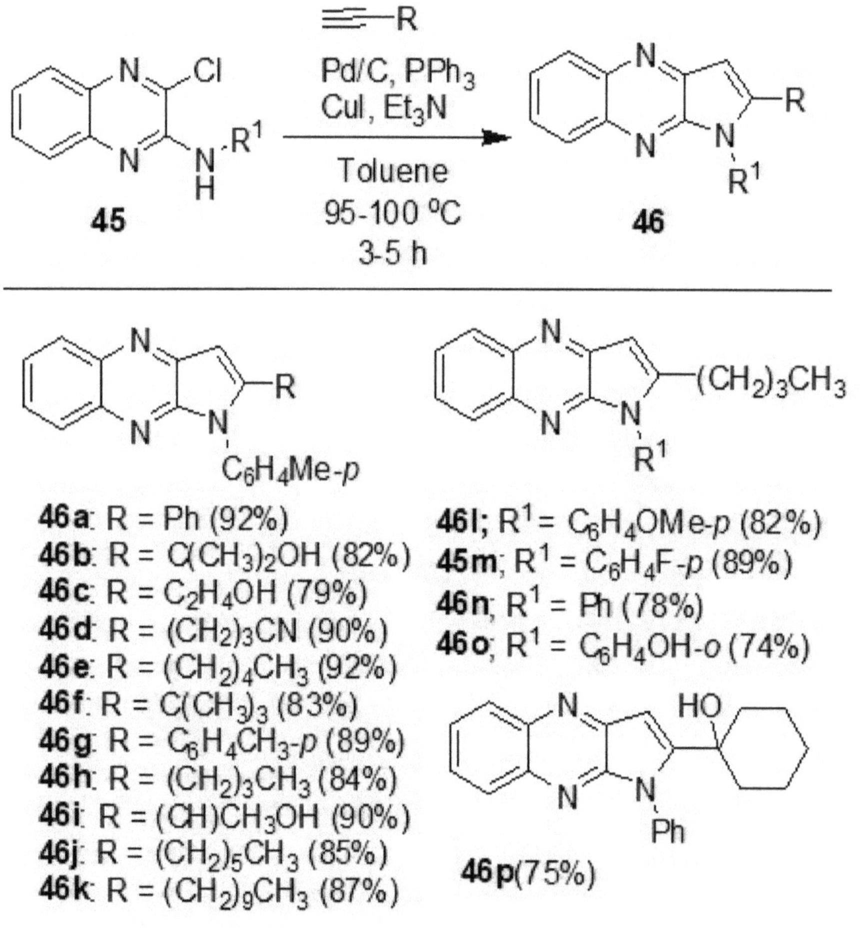

Pd/C, PPh3
CuI, Et3N
Toluene
95-100 °C
3-5 h
45
46
C6H4Me-p
(CH2)3CH3
46a: R = Ph (92%)
46b: R = C(CH3)2OH (82%)
46c: R = C2H4OH (79%)
46d: R = (CH2)3CN (90%)
46e: R = (CH2)4CH3 (92%)
46f: R = C(CH3)3 (83%)
46g: R = C6H4CH3-p (89%)
46h: R = (CH2)3CH3 (84%)
46i: R = (CH)CH3OH (90%)
46j: R = (CH2)5CH3 (85%)
46k: R = (CH2)9CH3 (87%)
46l; R1 = C6H4OMe-p (82%)
45m; R1 = C6H4F-p (89%)
46n; R1 = Ph (78%)
46o; R1 = C6H4OH-o (74%)
46p(75%)

Scheme 23. Synthesis of1,2-disubstituted pyrrolo[2,3-*b*]quinoxalines

It worthy to mention here that the amination of several halo *N*-heteroarenes using a large number of amines was successful when the reaction was performed in the presence of $InCl_3$ under microwave irradiation (in a pressure-tight microwave tube generally at ~ 120 ºC).[19a] Similarly AlCl$_3$ or transition metal / microwave irradiation free C-N bond forming reaction between chloropyridine and a variety of simple amides under refluxing conditions has been reported for the synthesis of aminopyridines.[19b]

CHAPTER XXV

Hydroarylation–heteroarylation in a single pot

A new strategy based on hydroarylation-heteroarylation process mediated by $AlCl_3$ in a single pot has been reported in 2013.[41] The methodology involved aromatic C–H bond addition to an alkyne and heteroarylation of an arene in the same pot leading to densely functionalized olefins, e.g. 2-(2,2-diarylvinyl)-3-arylquinoxalines. This class of compounds was designed as potential inhibitors of sirtuins. Notably, because of their up-regulation in various types of cancer, sirtuins are considered as promising targets for cancer therapeutics[42] and inhibition of sirtuins leads to reduced growth of cancer cells. The exploration of 2-(2,2-diarylvinyl)-3-arylquinoxalines as potential anticancer agents was inspired by activities of 3-enynyl flavones against a panel of cancer cell lines as reported earlier.[43] This anticipated sirtuin inhibitory properties was also supported by in silico studies. Thus the target compounds (**48**) were prepared by treating the 3-arylethynyl substituted 2-chloroquinoxaline derivatives (**47**) with a number of phenols in the presence of $AlCl_3$ (Scheme 24).[41] A representative compound showed promising activities against sirtuins (IC_{50} ~ 32.9 µM against mammalian SIRT1), no adverse effects when tested for toxicity in a zebrafish embryo in a range 10 nM–30 µM and inhibited cell growth human hepatocellular liver carcinoma (HepG2) cells at 50 µM.

48aa: ,R^1=H,R^2=H,R^3=OH (82%); **48ab:** R^1=H,R^2=CH$_3$,R^3=OH (79%); **47ac:** ,R^1=CH$_3$,R^2=H,R^3=OCH$_3$ (64%); **48ad:** ,R^1=CH$_3$,R^2=CH$_3$,R^3=OCH$_3$ (68%); **48ae:**R^1=Et,R^2=H,R^3=OEt (65%); **48af:** R^1=H,R^2=CH$_3$,R^3=H (62%); **48ag:** R^1=H,R^2=H,R^3=CH$_3$ (55%);

48ba:R^1=H,R^2=H,R^3=OH (80%); **48bb:** R^1=H,R^2=CH$_3$,R^3=OH (78%); **48bc:** R^1=CH$_3$,R^2=H,R^3=OCH$_3$ (73%); **48bd:**R^1=CH$_3$,R^2=CH$_3$,R^3=OCH$_3$ (71%); **48be:** R^1=Et,R^2=H,R^3=OEt (66%)

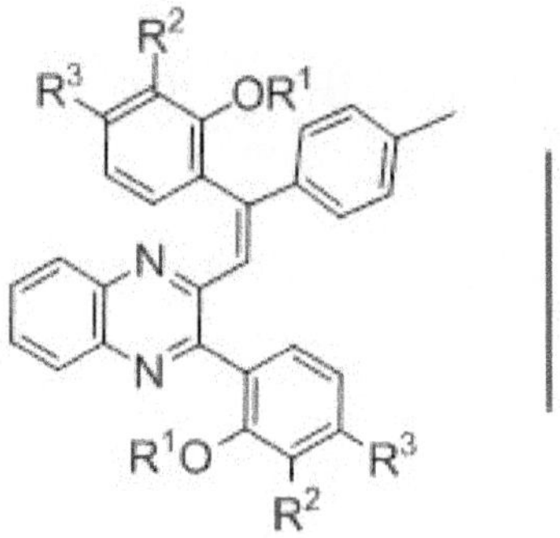

48ca:R^1=H,R^2=H,R^3=OH (71%); **48cb:** R^1=H,R^2=CH$_3$,R^3=OH (69%); **48cc:** R^1=CH$_3$,R^2=H,R^3=OCH$_3$ (63%); **48cd:**R^1=CH$_3$,R^2=CH$_3$,R^3=OCH$_3$ (67%); **48ce:** R^1=Et,R^2=H,R^3=OEt (58%); **48cf:** R^1=Et,R^2=CH$_3$,R^3=OEt (55%)

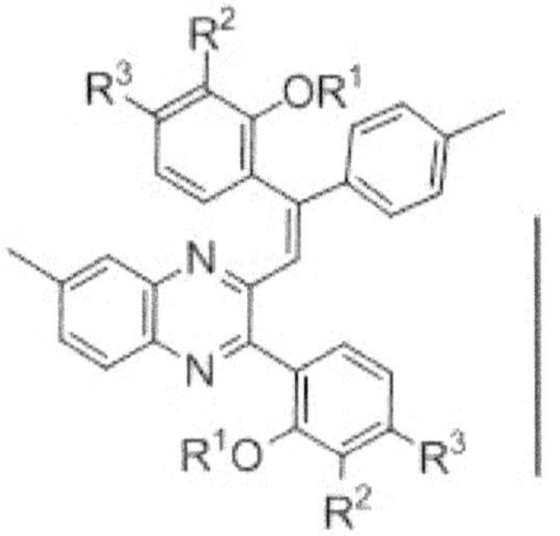

48da:R^1=H,R^2=H,R^3=OH (74%); **48db:** R^1=H,R^2=CH$_3$,R^3=OH (71%); **48dc:** R^1=CH$_3$,R^2=H,R^3=OCH$_3$ (64%); **48dd:**R^1=CH$_3$,R^2=CH$_3$,R^3=OCH$_3$ (60%); **48de:** R^1=Et,R^2=H,R^3=OEt (56%); **48df:** R^1=Et,R^2=CH$_3$,R^3=OEt (58%)

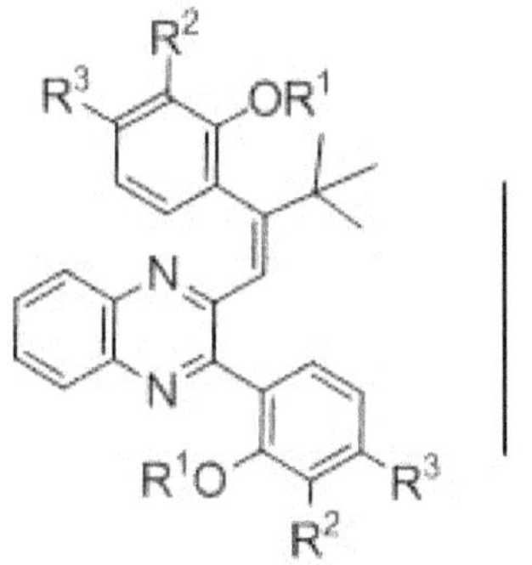

48ea:R^1=H,R^2=H,R^3=OH (55%); **48eb:**R^1=H,R^2=CH$_3$,R^3=OH (62%); **48ec:** R^1=CH$_3$,R^2=H,R^3=OCH$_3$ (60%); **48ed:**R^1=CH$_3$,R^2=CH$_3$,R^3=OCH$_3$ (63%); **48ee:** R^1=Et,R^2=H,R^3=OEt (61%).

Scheme 24. Synthesis of 2-(2,2-diarylvinyl)-3-arylquinoxaline

CHAPTER XXVI

Sulfonyl group migration for N–alkyl/aryl/heteroarylsulfonyl indoles

With the goal of identification of indole based CM inhibitors it was necessary to generate a variety of indole derivatives for *in vitro* screen. Accordingly it was unexpectedly observed that during C-3 acylation of *N*-alkyl/aryl/ heteroarylsulfonyl indoles (**49**) in the presence of AlCl$_3$ a regioselective sulfonyl group migration occurred to afford the functionalized new indoles (**50**) in which the nitrogen atom was unprotected and the sulfonyl group shifted to C-7 of the indole ring (Scheme 25).[44] A systematic study was performed to establish the optimal reaction conditions that subsequently applied to prepare a range of compounds. The N–S bond cleavage appeared to be aided by the bulky ^tBu group at C-2 resulting in the migration of the *N*-sulfonyl group. Moreover, a number of indoles underwent smooth N–S bond cleavage in the absence of acyl chloride leading to the C-7 sulfonyl substituted indoles indicating the key role played by AlCl$_3$ in this transformation. Several of these compounds were tested for their inhibitory potential against CM *in vitro*. Indeed, a representative compound showed inhibition and interactions with CM both *in vitro* and *in silico* studies.

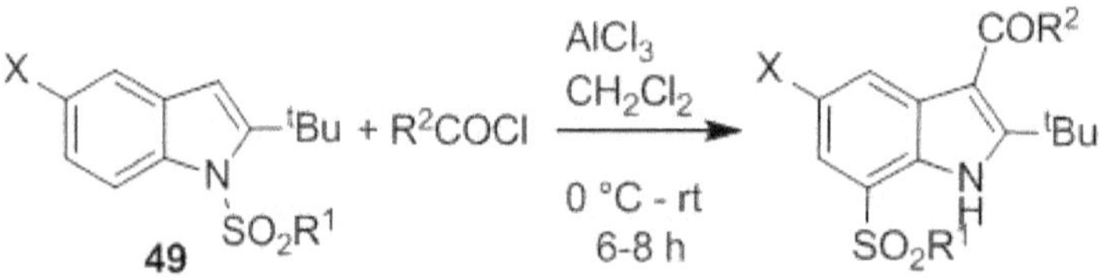

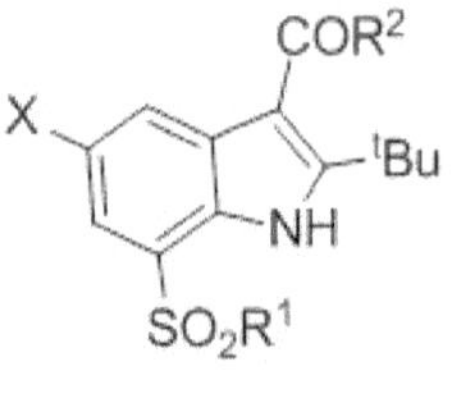

50a: X=Cl R^1=CH$_3$, R^2=CH$_3$ (70%); **50b:** X=Cl, R^1=CH$_3$, R^2=CH$_2$CH$_3$ (67%); **50c:** X=F, R^1=CH$_3$, R^2=CH$_3$ (68%); **50d:** X=F, R^1=CH$_3$, R^2=CH$_2$CH$_3$ (65%); **50e:** X=Br, R^1=CH$_3$, R^2=CH$_3$ (66%); **50f:** X=Br, R^1=CH$_3$, R^2=CH$_2$CH$_3$ (65%); **50g:** X=CH$_3$, R^1=CH$_3$, R^2=CH$_3$ (60%); **50h:** X=CH$_3$, R^1=CH$_3$, R^2=CH$_2$CH$_3$ (58%); **50i:** X=Cl, R^1=C$_6$H$_5$Me-*p*, R^2=CH$_3$ (58%); **50j:** X=Cl, R^1=C$_6$H$_5$Me-*p*, R^2=CH$_2$CH$_3$ (55%); **50k:** X=F, R^1=C$_6$H$_5$Me-*p*, R^2=CH$_3$ (56%); **50l:** X=CH$_3$, R^1=C$_6$H$_5$Me-*p*, R^2=CH$_3$ (52%)

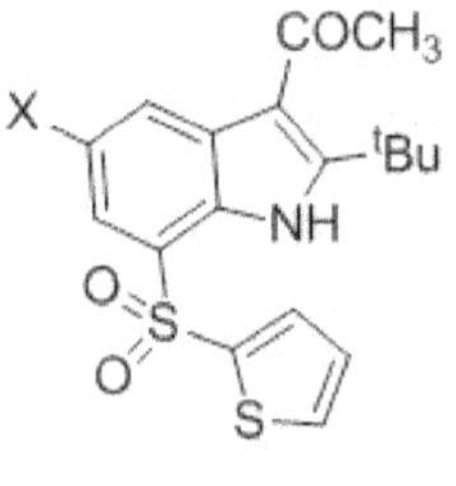

50m: X=Cl (55%); **50n:** X=F (58%); **50o:** X=Br (55%); **50p:** X=CH$_3$ (54%);

Scheme 25. Synthesis of 1-(2-alkyl-5-substituted-7-sulfonyl-1*H*-indol-3-yl)alkanone.

CHAPTER XXVII

Miscellaneous methods

There are some AlCl$_3$ mediated C-C bond forming reactions have been reported that do not belong to any category of reactions as presented in previous sections. One such example is arylation of 1,2,4-triazines in the presence of AlCl$_3$ where it was demonstrated that the C=N bond of a wide range of 1,2,4-triazines underwent addition of arenes.[45] More such interesting examples are presented in the following section.

Acylation of Csp^3

While methods for the synthesis of 3-(2-oxoalkyl)indoles were known in the literature many of these methods suffered from several drawbacks such as the use of either unstable diazo compounds or moisture-sensitive organometallic reagents or expensive catalysts. Interestingly, AlCl$_3$-induced acylation of 3-methylindole (**51**) afforded a novel route for the preparation of 3-(2-oxoalkyl)indoles (**52**) (Scheme 26).[46a] The product formation in this one-pot reaction was largely dependent on the conditions of the reaction employed. The methodology did not require protection-deprotection steps and was amenable for the scale-up synthesis of these indole derivatives. Notably, though the involvement of 3-methyl group was not ruled out the 2-acetyl-3-methylindole was obtained when 3-methylindole was treated with *N*-methylacetonitrilium fluoroborate followed by hydrolysis of the resulting imine salt.[46b]

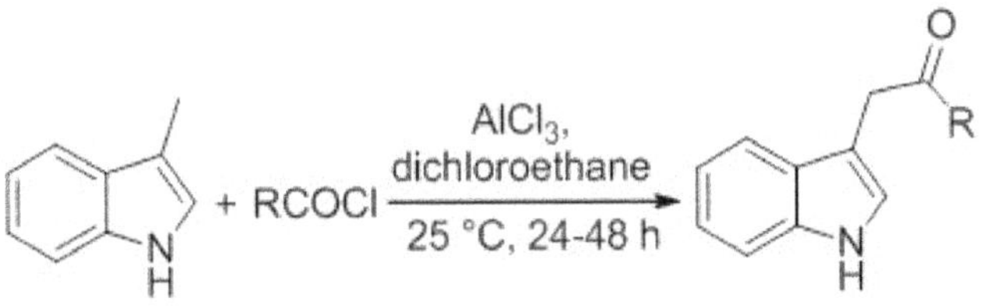

52a; R= CH$_3$ (58%), **52b**; R= C$_2$H$_5$ (54%), **52c**; R= C$_3$H$_7$ (36%), **52d**; R= C$_4$H$_9$ (66%), **52e** R= C$_5$H$_{11}$(69%), **52a**; R= C$_6$H$_{13}$ (50%), **52b**; R= C$_7$H$_{15}$ (72%), **52c**; R= CH$_2$CH$_2$-cyclopentane(56%),

Scheme 26. AlCl$_3$-Mediated Synthesis of 3-(2-Oxoalkyl)indoles

Diels–Alder reaction of furan with electron-deficient 3-carbethoxycoumarins

An interesting and one-pot synthesis of fused furo[3,2-*b*]pyranochroman-2-ones with multiple stereogenic centers was achieved by using an AlCl$_3$ mediated method. Thus Diels–Alder reaction of furan with electron-deficient 3-carbethoxycoumarins (**53**) gave the Michael-type adducts obtained from the rearrangement of the intermediate Diels–Alder adducts, instead of the Diels–Alder cycloadducts (**54**) (Scheme 27).[47] Trapping of the dipolar intermediate with electron-deficient aromatic aldehydes gave the desired fused furo[3,2-*b*]pyranochroman-2-ones (**55**, Scheme 28). Notably, the ring opening of the lactone moiety of compound **54** accomplished a facile route to generate diverse scaffolds.[47]

R2
R1
COOEt
53
AlCl3,neat, rt
20-24h
COOEt
54
54a: R1=H, R2=H (83%); 54b: R1=Br, R2=H (78%); 54c: R1=Cl, R2=H (80%);
54d: R1=F, R2=H (76%); 54e: R1=H, R2=OH (73%); 54f: R1=NO2, R2=H (75%)

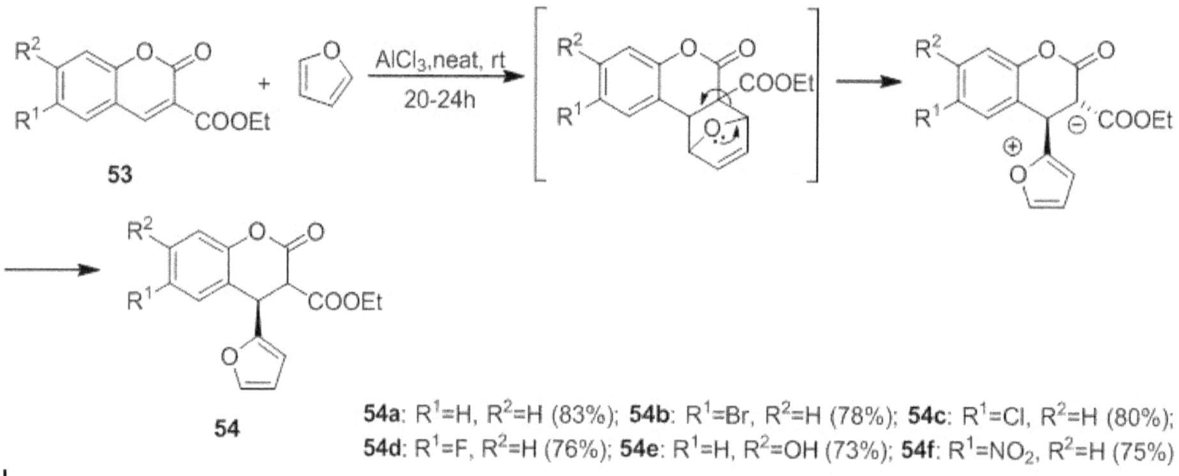

Scheme 27. Formation of Michael adducts from 3-carbethoxycoumarins with furan

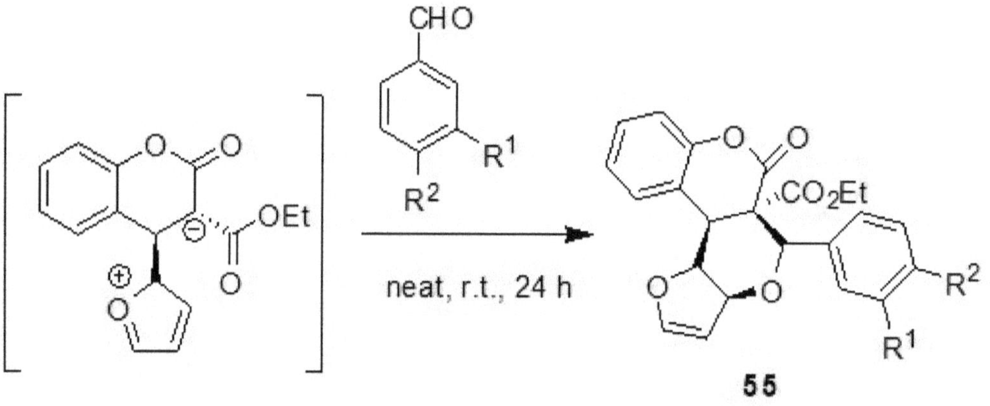

CHO
R1
R2
OEt
neat, r.t., 24 h
CO2Et
55

Scheme 28. Synthesis of fused furo[3,2-*b*]pyranochroman-2-ones.

Other C-C bond forming reactions

While not used directly for the synthesis of *N*-heteroarenes, there are other C-C bond forming reactions that could be useful for the preparation of building blocks leading to the biologically valuable *N*-heteroarenes. One such example is $AlCl_3$ catalyzed multicomponent reaction (MCR) that involved the reaction of enolizable ketones or alkyl acetoacetates with aldehydes, acetonitrile and acetyl chloride to afford β-acetamido ketone or ester derivatives in high to excellent yields.[48] This is perhaps a rare example of MCR catalysed by $AlCl_3$. In another strategy FC alkylation of various arenes/heteroarenes to *b*-nitrostyrenes mediated by $AlCl_3$ afforded either a-arylated nitroalkanes or a-arylated hydroximoyl chlorides depending on the reaction temperature used.[49] Similarly, FC alkylation of benzene with *α,β*-unsaturated amides[50a] and $AlCl_3$-mediated C-C bond-forming reaction of α-hydroxyketene-*S,S*-acetals with arenes has also been reported.[50b]

CHAPTER XXVIII

Conclusions

It is now evident that AlCl$_3$ mediated methods other than FC reactions as presented here have enormous potential for the synthesis of *N*-heteroarene based small molecules for different purposes. So far stoichiometric amount of AlCl$_3$ has been used in most of these cases and the reactions appeared to be less efficient when catalytic amount of AlCl$_3$ was used. Thus formation of gaseous HCl during the reaction and a significant amount of aluminum waste after the usual workup is a concern for these methodologies especially during the scale-up activities. For heteroarylation strategy, the reaction was found to be less effective unless the electron reach arenes/heteroarenes were employed. Indeed, this had narrowed down the scope of this methodology that also required the use of substrates containing a chloro bearing azomethine carbon [e.g. =C–C(Cl)=N–]. However, being inexpensive, less toxic and a strong Lewis acid, AlCl$_3$ appeared to be attractive as its uses in FC reactions even in industrial scale is well documented. Thus like FC reactions the AlCl$_3$-mediated methodologies as described above are expected to find industrial applications. Indeed, the AlCl$_3$-induced heteroarylation despite having some limitations could be viewed as a useful alternative to the transition metal mediated cross coupling processes such as Suzuki reactions (when applied to a similar type of C-C bond forming reaction) as the methodology avoids cumbersome preparation of boronic acids or other organometallic reagents and formation of homocoupled products as byproducts. Moreover, application potential of this methodology has already been demonstrated in medicinal and pharmaceutical chemistry. However, unlike FC reactions many of these AlCl$_3$ mediated methodologies are still in their initial stage of developments and a continuing effort to uncover their further potential in other areas of chemistry is necessary. Catalytic use of AlCl$_3$ or identification of alternative, recoverable and recyclable catalysts could be the way forward. Overall, the AlCl$_3$ mediated C-C bond forming reactions will continue to provide quick and direct access of novel and valuable *N*-heteroarenes the synthesis of which might be difficult by other means.

CHAPTER XXIX

References

1. Gomtsyan, A. Chem Heterocycl Comp (2012) 48: 7. doi:10.1007/s10593-012-0960-z

2. Heterocyclic Chemistry in Drug Discovery, Li, J. J., Ed.; John *Wiley* & Sons: Hoboken, NJ USA, 2013, ISBN: 978-1-118-14890-7.

3. **I. Nakamura; Y. Yamamoto, Transition-Metal-Catalyzed Reactions in Heterocyclic Synthesis. Chem. Rev., 2004, *104* (5), pp 2127–2198**

4. N. Miyaura, A. Suzuki, Palladium-Catalyzed Cross-Coupling Reactions of Organoboron Compounds. Chem. Rev., **1995**, *95* (7), pp 2457–2483

5. (a) Negishi, E.-i.; Luo, F.-T.; Frisbee, R.; Matsushita, H. *Heterocycles* **1982**, *18*, 117-122. (b) Gauthier, D. R.; Szumigala, R. H.; Dormer, P. G.; Armstrong, J. D.; Volante, R. P.; Reider, P. J. *Org. Lett.* **2002**, *4*, 375-378. (c) Applications of Transition Metal Catalysis in Drug Discovery and Development: An Industrial Perspective, Crawley, M. L.; Trost, B. M.; Eds.: John *Wiley* & Sons, New York, NY, *2012*, 376 pp, ISBN: 978-0-470-63132-4

6. For representative examples, see: (a) S. Wu, H. Ma, Z. Lei, Tetrahedron 66 (2010) 8641-8647; (b) Hu, X.; Chuah, G. K. H.; Jaenicke, S. *Appl. Catal. A: General* **2001**, *217*, 1. (c) Abdayem, R.; Baccolini, G.; Boga, C.; Monari, M.; Selva, S. *Tetrahedron Lett.* **2003**, *44*, 2649; (d) Groves, J. K. *Chem. Soc. Rev.* **1972**, *1*, 73; (e) Gattermann, L.; Koch, J. A. *Ber.* **1897**, *30*, 1622; (f) Karade, N. N.; Shirodkar, S. G.; Potrekar, R. A.; Karade, H. N. *Synth. Commun.* **2004**, *34*, 391; (g) Piao, C. R.; Zhao, Y. L.; Han, X. D.; Liu, Q. *J. Org. Chem.* **2008**, *73*, 2264; (h) Shen, J.; Huang, Z.; Li, J.; Gao, L.; Zhou, H.; Qian, Y. *Carbon* **2005**, *43*, 2823.

7. (a) Friedel, C.; Crafts, J. M. (1877) "Sur une nouvelle méthode générale de synthèse d'hydrocarbures, d'acétones, etc.," *Compt. Rend.*, **84**: 1392 & 1450; (b) <u>N. O. Calloway</u>, The Friedel-Crafts Syntheses. Chem. Rev., 1935, 17 (3), pp 327–392.

8. (a) G. Illuminati, H. Gilman, J. Am. Chem. Soc., 1952, 74, 2896–2899 (b) Pollak, A.; Stanovnik, B.; Tisler, M. Synthesis of Pyridazine Derivatives. XII. Friedel—Crafts Reaction with 3,6-Dichloropyridazine. *J. Org. Chem.* 1966, 31, 4297-4298; (c) Coates, W. J.; McKillop, A. J. Org. Chem. 1990, 55, 5418.

9. M. W. Khan and N. G. Kundu, J. Chem. Res. (S) 1999, 99, 20-21; **DOI:** 10.1039/A806787B

10. Akahane, A.; Katayama, H.; Mitsunaga, T.; Kato, T.; Kinoshita, T.; Kita, Y.; Kusunoki, T.; Terai, T.; Yoshida, K.; Shiokawa, Y. J. Med. Chem. 1999, 42, 779

11. M. Pal, V. R. Batchu, S. Khanna, K. R. Yeleswarapu, *Tetrahedron*2002, 58, 9933

12. Yamaguchi, M.; Kamei, K.; Koga, T.; Akima, M.; Kuroki, T.; Ohi, N. *J. Med. Chem.* **1993**, *36*, 4052.

13. (a) Pal, M.; Batchu, V. R.; Parasuraman, K.; Yeleswarapu, K, R. *J. Org. Chem.* **2003**, *68*, 6806; (b) Knopfel, T. F.; Aschwanden, P.; Ichikawa, T.; Watanabe, T.; Carreira, E. M. *Angew. Chem. Int. Ed.* 2004, 43, 5971; (c) S. Fujimori, T. F. Knöpfel, P. Zarotti, T. Ichikawa, D. Boyall, E. M. Carreira, *Bull. Chem. Soc. Jpn.* **2007**80, 1635-1657; (d) Kaila N, Huang A, Moretto A, Follows B, Janz K, Lowe M, Thomason J, Mansour TS, Hubeau C, Page K, Morgan P, Fish S, Xu X, Williams C, Saiah E., Diazine indole acetic acids as potent, selective, and orally bioavailable antagonists of chemoattractant receptor homologous molecule expressed on Th2 cells (CRTH2) for the treatment of allergic inflammatory diseases. J Med Chem. 2012, 55, 5088-109. (e) G. R. Dhage, S. R. Deshmukh and S. R. Thopate, *RSC Adv.*, 2015,5, 33377-33384.

14. (a) Pal, M.; Batchu, V. R.; Dager, I.; Swamy, N, K.; Padakanti, S. *J. Org. Chem.* **2005**, *70*, 2376. (b) Pal, M.; Alexander, C. W.; Khanna, I.; Iqbal, J.; Pillarisetti, R.; Maitra, S.; Roberts, G. W.; Sagi, L.; Krishna, C. V.; Sreenu, J. Novel pyridine compounds, process for their preparation and composition containing them. *US Patent Application* US 2006/0084644 A1, 20 April 2006.

15. C. Gosmini, C. Bassene-Ernst, M. Durandetti, Synthesis of functionalized 2-arylpyridines from 2-halopyridines and various aryl halides via a nickel catalysis. *Tetrahedron 2009, 65, 6141-6146*

16. Kodimuthali, A.; Nishad, T. C.; Prasunamba. P. L.; Pal. M. *Tetrahedron Letters*, **2009**, *50*, 354.

17. Kodimuthali, A.; Chary. B. C.; Prasunamba. P. L.; Pal. M. *Tetrahedron Letters*, **2009**,*50*, 1618.

18. (a) Kumar, S.; Sahu, D. P. *J. Heterocyclic Chem*, **2009**, *46*, 748; (b) Kumar, S.; Shakya, N.; Gupta, S.; Sarkar, J.; Sahu, D, P. *Bioorg. Med. Chem. Lett.*, **2009**, *19*, 2542. (c) Pal, M.; Khanna, I.; Subramanian, V.; Padakanti, S.; Pillarisetti, S. World Patent Application WO 2006/058201 A2, June 1, 2006.

19. (a) Staderini, M., Bolognesi, M. L. and Menéndez, J. C. (2015), Lewis Acid-Catalyzed Generation of C-C and C-N Bonds on π-Deficient Heterocyclic Substrates. Adv. Synth. Catal., 357: 185–195. (b) A. Kodimuthali; A. Mungara; P. L. Prasunamba; M. Pal, J. Braz. Chem. Soc., 2010, 21, 1439-1445.

20. Pal, M.; Rao, Y. K.; Khanna, I.; Swamy, N. K.; Subramanian, V.; Batchu, V. R.; Iqbal, J.; Pillarisetti, S. U. S. Patent Application US 2006/0128729 A1, June 15, 2006.

21. (a) Modica, M.; Santagati, M.; Guccione, S.; Russo, F.; Cagnotto, A.; Goegan, M.; Mennini, T. Eur. J. Med. Chem. 2000, 35, 1065; (b) Modica, M.; Romeo, G.; Materia, L.; Russo, F.; Cagnotto, A.; Mennini, T.; Gaspar, R.; Falkay, G.; Fulop, F. Bioorg. Med. Chem. 2004, 12, 3891.

22. Kumar, K. S.; Chamakuri, S.; Iqbal, J.; Pal, M. *Tetrahedron Letters* 2010, *51*, 3269.

23. (a) Hocek, M.; Holy, A; Votruba, I; Dvorakova, H. J. Med. Chem. 2000, 43, 1817. (b) Gundersen, L. L; Nissen-Meyer, J.; Rise, F.; Spilsberg, B. J. Med. Chem. 2002, 45, 1383. (c) Bakkestuen, A. K.; Gundersen, L. L.; Utenova, B. T. J. Med. Chem. 2005, 48, 2710. (d) Hocek, M.; Naus, P.; Pohl, R; Votruba, I.; Furman, P. A.; Tharnish, P. M.; Otto, M. J. J. Med. Chem. 2005, 48, 5869.

24. Guo, H. M.; Li. P.; Niu. H. Y.; Wang. D. C.; Qu, G. R. *J. Org. Chem.*, **2010**, *75* (17), pp 6016–6018

25. (a) Hulme, C.; Moriarty, K.; Miller, B.; Mathew, R.; Ramanjulu, M.; Cox, P.; Souness, J.; Page, K. M.; Uhl, J.; Travis, J.; Huang, F.-C.; Labaudiniere, R.; Djuric, S. W. Bioorg. Med. Chem. Lett. 1867, 1998, 8; (b) Buckley, G. M.; Cooper, N.; Dyke, H. J.; Galleway, F.; Gowers, L.; Haughan, A. F.; Kendall, H. J.; Lowe, C.; Maxey, R.; Montana, J. G.; Naylor, R.; Oxford, J.; Peake, J. C.; Picken, C. L.; Runcie, K. A.; Sabin, V.; Sharpe, A.; Warneck, J. B. H. Bioorg. Med. Chem. Lett. 2002, 12, 1613; (c) Billah, M.; Buckley, G. M.; Cooper, N.; Dyke, H. J.; Egan, R.; Ganguly, A.; Gowers, L.; Haughan, A. F.; Kendall, H. J.; Lowe, C.; Minnicozzi, M.; Montana, J. G.; Oxford, J.; Peake, J. C.; Picken, C. L.; Piwinski, J. J.; Naylor, R.; Sabin, V.; Shih, N.-Y.; Warneck, J. B. H. Bioorg. Med. Chem. Lett. 2002, 12, 1617; (d) Kodimuthali, A.; Jabaris, S. S. L.; Pal, M. J. Med. Chem. 2008, 51, 5471;

26. K. S. Kumar.; S. K. Kumar.; Y. Sreenivas B.; G. D. Rao.; R. Kapavarapu.; D. Rambabu.; G. R. Krishna.; C. M. Reddy.; K. V. L. Parsa, M. Pal.*Bioorg. Med. Chem.* **2012**, *20*, 2199.

27. (a) Badran, M. M.; Abonzid, K. A.; Hussein, M. H. Arch. Pharm. Res. 2003, 26, 107; (b) 6. Singh, D. P.; Deivedi, S. K.; Hashim, S. R.; Singhal, R. G. Pharmaceuticals 2010, 3, 2416; (c) Al-Hiari, Y. M.; Qaisi, A. M.; El-Abadelah, M. M.; Voelter, W. *Monatshefte fur Chemie* 2006, 137, 243.

28. K. S. Kumar.; D. Rambabu,; S. Sandra,; R. Kapavarapu.; G. R. Krishna.; B. Rao.; M.V. Chatti.; K., C. M. Reddy.; P. Misra.; M. Pal. *Bioorg. Med. Chem.* **2012**, *20*, 1711.

29. (a) Walsh, C. T.; Liu, J.; Rusnak, F.; Sakaitani, M. Chem. Rev. 1990, 90, 1105; (b) Haslam, E. Shikimic Acid: Metabolism and Metabolites; Wiley: New York, 1993. (c) J. Cogo, V. Kaplum, D. P. Sangi, T. Ueda-Nakamura, A. G. Corrêa, C. V. Nakamura, Synthesis and biological evaluation of novel 2,3-disubstituted quinoxaline derivatives as antileishmanial and antitrypanosomal agents. European J. Med. Chem. 2015, 90, 107–123

30. K. S. Kumar, D. Rambabu, B. Prasad, M. Mujahid, G. R. Krishna, M. V. B. Rao, C. M. Reddy, G. R. Vanaja, A. M. Kalle and M. Pal, *Org. Biomol. Chem.*, 2012, 10, 4774

31. K. A. Nolan, D. J. Timson, I. J. Stratforda and R. A. Bryce, Bioorg. Med. Chem. Lett., 2006, 16, 6246.

32. K. S. Kumar, B. Bhaskar,M. S. Ramulu, N. P. Kumar, M. A. Ashfaq and M. Pal *Org. Biomol. Chem.*, 2017, 15, 82-87

33. K. S. Kumar.; R. Adepu.; R. Kapavarapu.; D. Rambabu.; G. R. Krishna; C. M. Reddy.; K. K. Priya.; K. V. L. Parsa.; M. Pal. *Tetrahedron Lett.* **2012**, *53*, 1134.

34. C. Neagoie, E. Vedrenne, F. Buron, J. Y. M´erour, S. Rosca, S. Bourg, O. Lozach, L. Meijer, B. Baldeyrou, A. Lansiaux and S. Routier, Eur. J. Med. Chem., 2012, 49, 379.

35. K. S. Kumar, S. R. Meesa, B. Rajeshama, B. Bhaskera, M. A. Ashfaq, A. A. Khan, S.S. Rao, M. Pal,*RSC Adv.*, **2016**, 6, 48324.

36. Keivanloo, A.; Bakherad, M.; Rahimi, A.; Taheri, S. A. N. Tetrahedron Lett. 2010, 51, 2409.

37. A. Nakhi, M. S. Rahman, R. Kishore, C. L. T. Meda, G. S. Deora, K. V. L. Parsa and M. Pal, Bioorg. Med. Chem. Lett., 2012, 22, 6433.

38. P. V. Babu, S. Mukherjee, G. S. Deora, K. S. Chennubhotla, R. Medisetti, S. Yellanki, P. Kulkarni, S. Sripelly, K. V. L. Parsa, K. Chatti, K. Mukkanti and M. Pal, *Org. Biomol. Chem.*, 2013, 11, 6680.

39. (a) Desplat, V.; Geneste, A.; Begorre, M. A.; Fabre, S. B.; Brajot, S.; Massip, S.; Thiolat, D.; Mossalayi, D.; Jarry, C.; Guillon, J. J. Enzyme Inhib. Med. Chem. 2008, 23, 648; (b) Desplat, V.; Moreau, S.; Gay, A.; Fabre, S. B.; Thiolat, D.; Massip, S.; Macky, G.; Godde, F.; Mossalayi, D.; Jarry, C.; Guillon, J. J. Enzyme Inhib. Med. Chem. 2010, 25, 204.

40. B. Prasad, K.S. Kumar, P.V. Babu, K. Anusha, D. Rambabu, A. Kandale, G.R. Vanaja, A.M. Kalle, M. Pal, *Tetrahedron Lett.* 53 (2012) 6059-6066.

41. A. Nakhi, S. Archana, G. P. K. Seerapu, K. S. Chennubhotla, K. L. Kumar, P. Kulkarni, D. Haldar, M. Pal *Chem. Commun.*, **2013**, *49*, 6268

42. (a) S. Michan and D. Sinclair, Biochem. J., 2007, 404, 1; (b) A. Bedalov, T. Gatbonton, W. P. Irvine, D. E. Gottschling and J. A. Simon, Proc. Natl. Acad. Sci. U. S. A., 2001, 98, 15113.

43. M. Pal, R. Dakarapu, K. Parasuraman and V. Subramanian, J. Org. Chem., 2005, 70, 7179.

44. B. Prasad, R Adepu, S. Sandra, D. Rambabu, G. R. Krishna, C. M. Reddy, G. S. Deora, P. Misra, M. Pal *Chem. Commun.*, **2012**, *48*, 10434.

45. I. N. Egorov, Zeitschrift für Naturforschung B. 2014, 69, 899–905, doi: https://doi.org/10.5560/znb.2014-4103

46. (a) Pal, M., Dakarapu, R., Padakanti, S. *J. Org. Chem.* **2004**, *69*, 2913. (b) R. G. Giles, H. Heaney, M. J. Plater, Tetrahedron2015, 71, 7367–7385

47. Prabhakar, M.; Reddy, G. N.; Srinu, G.; Prasad. J. V.; Kumar, S. P.; Srinivas, O.; Iqbal, J.; Kumar, K. A. *Synlett,***2010**, 0947.

48. Mohammad Ali, Z., Ardeshir, K., Mohammad, M., Abdolkarim, Z., Maliheh, S., Fatemeh, D.-P., Hassan, K., Ahmad, A. D.-F. and Maria, M., Efficient Synthesis of β-Acetamido Ketones and Esters Using Aluminum Chloride as an Inexpensive and Green Catalyst. Chin. J. Chem., 2012, 30: 345–352. doi:10.1002/cjoc.201180460

49. Z. Tu, B. R. Raju, T.-R. Liou, V. Kavala, C.-W. Kuo, Y. Jang, Y.-H. Shih, C.-C. Wang, C.-F. Yao, Tetrahedron **2009**, *65*, 2436–2442.

50. (a) Koltunov, K. Y.; Walspurger, S.; Sommer, J. Tetrahedron Lett. 2004, 45, 3547–3549. (b) Piao, C.-R.; Zhao, Y.-L.; Han, X.-D.; Liu, Q. J. Org. Chem. 2008, 73, 2264–2269.